WEEKEND
WOOD
WORKER

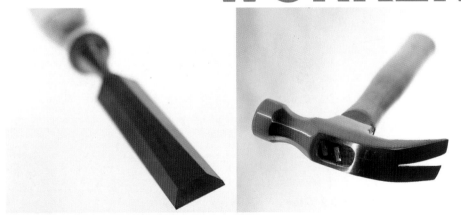

WEEKEND
WOOD
WORKER

18 STYLISH DESIGNS FOR WOODEN FURNITURE, WITH STEP-BY-STEP INSTRUCTIONS

STEPHEN CORBETT

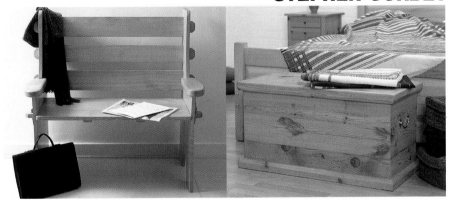

HERMES
HOUSE

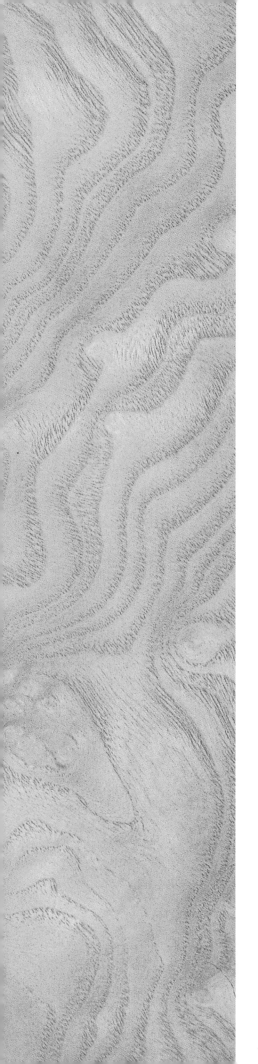

This edition is published by Hermes House

Hermes House is an imprint of Anness Publishing Ltd
Hermes House, 88–89 Blackfriars Road, London SE1 8HA
tel. 020 7401 2077; fax 020 7633 9499; info@anness.com

A CIP catalogue record for this book is available from the British Library.

Publisher: Joanna Lorenz
Managing Editor: Judith Simons
Senior Editor: Doreen Palamartschuk
Art Manager: Clare Reynolds
Designer: James Lawrence
Photographer: John Freeman
Illustrator: Julian Baker
Production Controller: Claire Rae

Previously published as *The Creative Woodworker Project Book*

1 3 5 7 9 10 8 6 4 2

Publisher's note

The author and the publisher have made every effort to ensure that
all instructions contained in this book are accurate and that the safest methods are recommended. The
publisher and author cannot accept liability for any injury, damage or
loss to persons or property as a result of using any tools in this book or carrying out any of the
projects. Before you begin any woodworking task, you should know how to use all your tools and
equipment safely and make sure you are confident about what you are doing.

Contents

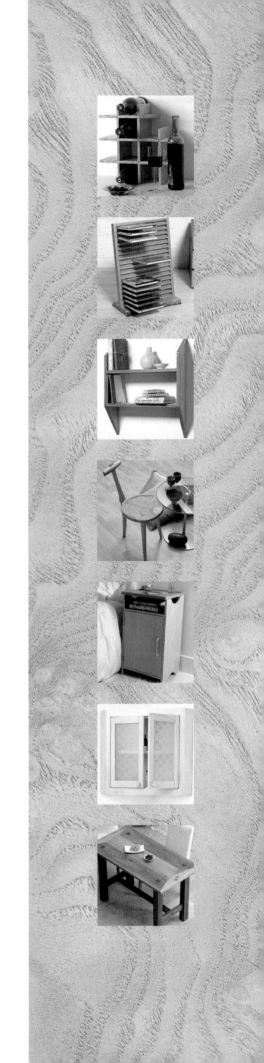

INTRODUCTION

MILLIONS OF PEOPLE SHARE A PASSIONATE INTEREST IN WOOD AND WOODWORKING, and despite the undoubted progress made by man in the development of metals, alloys, synthetic resins and plastics, wood remains the only truly tactile, practical material for furniture and do-it-yourself projects. And if properly looked after, wood will last for many years, as an examination of your surroundings will quickly confirm. Making furniture and other items in wood will not only provide you with an enjoyable and rewarding hobby, but also make you part of a tradition of craftsmanship that will always be with us.

Working with wood is an immensely satisfying pastime; the material is user-friendly and versatile. It rarely requires expensive and complicated machinery to be worked, and it feels warm and alive to the touch, as well as looking attractive at the same time. Wood is very strong for its weight and relatively inexpensive too. So it is the ideal material for the do-it-yourselfer who wants to expand his or her horizons and do something more ambitious than simply adding a few new shelves to an alcove or nailing up a bit of fencing in the garden.

While there is no substitute for experience and skill when making anything from raw materials, it is surprising what can be achieved with care and perseverance. Wood,

Above This table was finished with several coats of clear lacquer, rubbing down carefully between each coat for a mirror finish.
Left Enhance a simple, but elegant mirror frame by adding a narrow bevel around the edge of the glass.
Opposite Wood is strong, attractive and in furniture joints can be used as a decorative feature in a design.

particularly softwood, is easily worked and often needs only a modicum of hand tools. Beginners and the relatively inexperienced woodworker can turn out attractive, usable pieces of work, while the material's "friendliness" and familiarity positively encourage experimentation.

It is important to remember that the type and condition of the wood, the tools and techniques employed, the design principles and the basic safety rules that go with them all affect the finished product. Taking short-cuts and making choices without exploring all the options can produce quicker results, but home woodworking is not a race against time. Patience is one of the primary attributes of any good craftsperson.

The secret of being a successful woodworker lies in understanding that wood, as an organic material, was once alive, and that it can "live" again when shaped and formed by hand. Appreciating the variation in types of wood will allow you to make the most of the material's natural qualities.

The purpose of this book

Deciding that you want to make something from wood is one thing; deciding *what* to make is quite another. The very versatility of wood makes any number of projects possible, and items of furniture are the most obvious choice. However, unless you are a designer or have a natural ability to visualize your ideas and to work out how to make them, you are likely to fall at the first hurdle.

One possibility is to attempt to copy an existing item of furniture, perhaps from a picture in a book or a magazine, or from an actual example. But this still presents the task of selecting the most suitable materials and choosing

appropriate construction methods. For the experienced, skilled woodworker or furniture maker that may not be so much of a problem; for the less experienced, however, it can lead to serious pitfalls. That's where this book comes in, by providing you with a selection of useful wood-working projects.

All of the projects in this book are suitable for the home woodworker, and range from simple, everyday household items to quite sophisticated pieces of furniture. They have been specially designed, made and photographed, and you will find all the information you need to re-create them. On the other hand, if you feel confident enough, you can adapt the design and construction principles to suit your own ideas.

No two items made in wood are ever exactly the same, and that is the way it should be. No woodworker is ever completely satisfied with the latest project either – the next one will always be better. There is no substitute for experience, and that is what you will find distilled in

these pages. What you will not find is the reward that comes from your own efforts – the key to this lies in your own hands, and an understanding of the tools and materials you use.

Making accurate measurements is one of the most important skills to acquire if you want to achieve good results. The task can be made more confusing by the fact that different countries and suppliers of wood work to different standards, using either the metric or imperial system (or sometimes a combination of the two), when sizing the raw material.

The same applies to tool manufacturers and suppliers of fixings and hardware. The way through this maze is to develop an understanding of both systems until mental conversion becomes second nature. A pocket calculator may be of help, but on occasion, you may find that it actually slows the process.

In this book, dimensions are given in both metric and imperial form, but you should always check that the accuracy of any conversion is sufficient for the task in hand. Fractions of an inch, or 1 or 2 millimetres, either way are less critical in gauging large quantities of wood than when setting out detail, and converted values are often rounded up or down to make life easier. Whatever you do, always work in one system or the other, never a combination of the two. The table shown below provides some useful conversion factors and short-cut methods for estimating large quantities of wood.

Conversion table

Multiply	by	to obtain	short-cuts
inches	25.4	millimetres	divide by four and add two zeros (4in = 100mm)
feet	305	millimetres	multiply by three and add two zeros (1ft = 300mm)
square feet	0.093	square metres	divide by ten
cubic feet	0.028	cubic metres	divide by 35 (35cu ft = 1cu metre)
lb/cu ft	16.05	kg/cu m	add two zeros, divide by six
pounds	0.45	kilograms	divide by two and subtract 10% (2.2lb = 1kg)

PROJECTS

All of the following projects were produced specifically for this book, to give you a flying start in the principles of design and construction. You will need some woodworking skills, but whatever your level of expertise, there is sure to be something here to engage your imagination.

There are 18 well-crafted, practical wooden projects to choose from, with drawings and step-by-step instructions that will help you hone and develop your woodworking skills. To gain confidence, you can start with the simple and quick-to-make magazine rack and the classic picture or mirror frame. Or, if you already have skills, try the elegant low ash table or the sturdy and practical storage chest made from reclaimed wood. For more advanced woodworkers there are more intricate projects such as the solid butcher's block with a laminated maple top and the beautiful and strikingly-designed elm and teak dining table.

MAGAZINE RACK

THIS FOLDING RACK TAKES little time to construct and uses a few basic techniques. There are no joints to make, and no expensive tools are required; all you need are the basics of accurate marking out, cutting and fitting together. The materials are easy to obtain and are ready to use without further preparation. The interlocking design allows the rack to be opened up or folded flat and stowed away, with no need for clips or catches.

Materials

- 4.2m (14ft) of 75 x 12mm (3 x ½in) planed softwood for the slats
- 2.7m (9ft) of 50 x 25mm (2 x 1in) planed softwood for the legs
- 6mm (¼in) MDF (medium-density fiberboard) for the template
- 16 25mm (1in) brass wood screws
- 2 50mm (2in) brass wood screws
- Panel pin (brad)
- 2 65mm (2½in) coachbolts (carriage bolts), nuts and washers
- Thin cord

Fig. 11.1 Magazine rack

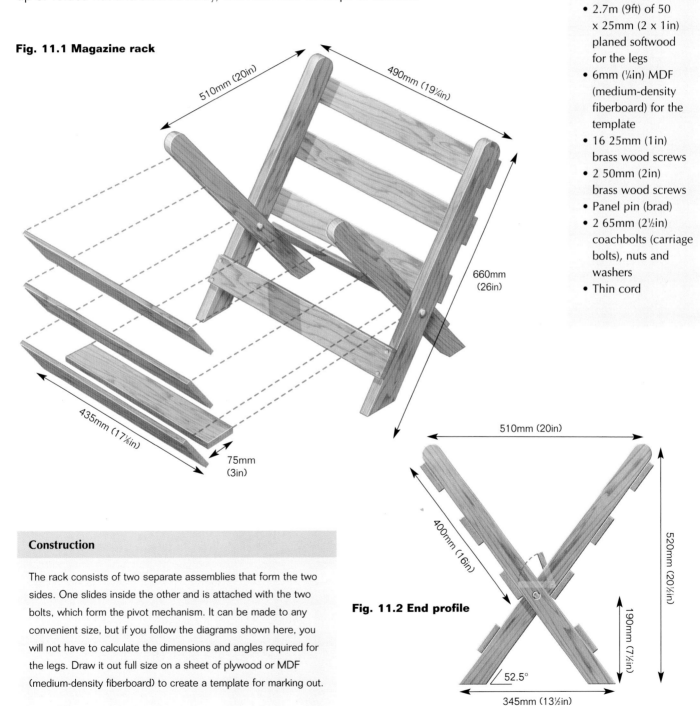

510mm (20in)

490mm (19¼in)

660mm (26in)

435mm (17⅛in)

75mm (3in)

Fig. 11.2 End profile

510mm (20in)

400mm (16in)

520mm (20½in)

190mm (7½in)

52.5°

345mm (13½in)

Construction

The rack consists of two separate assemblies that form the two sides. One slides inside the other and is attached with the two bolts, which form the pivot mechanism. It can be made to any convenient size, but if you follow the diagrams shown here, you will not have to calculate the dimensions and angles required for the legs. Draw it out full size on a sheet of plywood or MDF (medium-density fiberboard) to create a template for marking out.

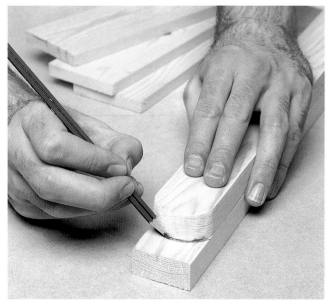

1 Cut the legs and the slats to their overall length. The slats for the inner frame are 55mm (2⅛in) shorter than those used for the outer frame, allowing them to easily slide within the latter. Cut a rounded profile at the top of each leg if desired, using the first as a pattern for the others so that they will be uniform.

2 Lay each pair of legs in turn over the template you have drawn out on a sheet of MDF and mark the positions of the slats and pivot point. Support the upper leg with a small offcut (scrap) of wood to keep it level. Drill a small pilot hole through the pivot point of each leg at this stage.

3 Assemble the inner frame. Insert one screw at each end of the top slat, then use a try square to adjust the assembly before you proceed. It is essential that the frames are absolutely square. Make sure the ends of the slats do not protrude over the sides of the frame.

4 Add the third slat, then turn the frame over to attach the bottom slat. The final assembly will be easier if you omit the second slat at this stage; it can be added when the rack is bolted together. Three slats are sufficient at this stage to keep the assembly square.

5 Use the inner frame as a building jig for the outer frame. Position the components carefully, making sure that the pivot holes are in line. Insert a small panel pin to keep the legs aligned in the correct position as you work. Note how the angled ends of the legs face in opposite directions.

6 Use two small offcuts of 12mm (½in) wood at each side to support the outer legs at the correct level. Screw the top and third slats in place, checking they are square as before. All four legs should be parallel to allow the assembly to move freely.

7 Turn the assembly over to fit the bottom slat. At this stage, the two frames should enclose each other, but they can still be slid apart if required. Now is a good time to clean up any rough edges with medium-grade sandpaper before proceeding. You could also apply a coat of clear sealer or varnish.

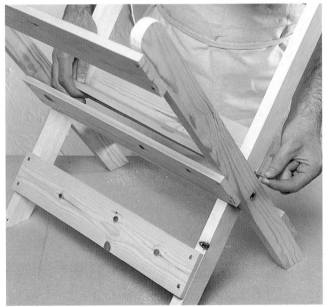

8 Drill through the legs for the coachbolts, using the pilot holes to guide the drill bit. Fit a coachbolt to each side, inserting a large washer between the moving parts to reduce friction. Fit the nuts on the inside, but do not over-tighten them or you will distort the framework. Note how the bottom slat on the outer frame will act as a stop to hold the rack in the open position.

9 Insert the bottom piece, which acts as a floor for the rack. Cut it to fit between the legs of the inner frame and attach with two long brass screws. It should pivot easily, allowing the rack to be folded flat for storage. Put in the remaining two slats. Add a couple of lengths of thin cord between the bottom slats as a final touch to secure the legs in their open position.

WINE RACK

Materials

- 760 x 600mm
  (30 x 24in) of
  12mm (½in)
  birch plywood

THIS SIMPLE PROJECT WILL PROVIDE practice in handling a few basic tools and learning one of the most important skills in woodwork – cutting straight and accurately to form simple halving (half) joints. It is made from birch-faced plywood, which can be attractive in its own right, and is finished with clear lacquer to seal it.

Construction

There are six components to this project, but only two different panel sizes. The sole critical dimension is the width of each compartment, which must suit your chosen wine bottle – 90mm (3½in) is a typical size.

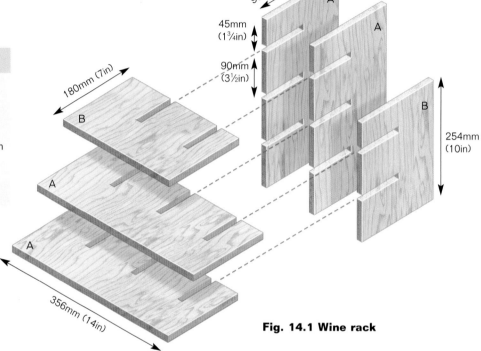

Fig. 14.1 Wine rack

Dimensions shown: 90mm (3½in), 45mm (1¾in), 90mm (3½in), 180mm (7in), 254mm (10in), 356mm (14in); panels labelled A and B.

1 Cut the panels to size (see diagram above) with a crosscut panel saw or jigsaw, making sure that all are square. When cutting across the end grain of plywood, you will obtain a much neater finish by scoring along the cut line with a knife to prevent the saw from splintering the outer layer of ply.

2 Firmly clamp each panel upright in a vice and trim down to the scored lines with a smoothing plane to produce neat, square edges all round. Finish off with medium sandpaper wrapped around a sanding block, using long, smooth strokes to keep the edges straight and square.

3 Set out the lines for each slot as shown, using the dimensions given in the diagram. Draw along each side of a small offcut (scrap) of plywood to establish the correct slot width without measuring each time. Use the first panel as a template for marking out the others.

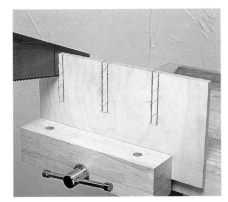

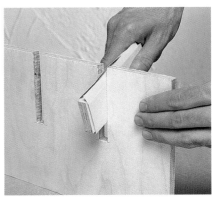

4 Clamp each panel vertically and cut downward carefully, keeping to the waste side of each line. A sharp panel saw will be more controllable than a power saw for making accurate cuts of this kind.

5 Use a mallet and a 12mm (½in) chisel to tap down at the ends of the slots. Each slot should extend to half the width of the panel so that the two halves of the joint slide together and leave the edges of the panels flush.

6 Wrap a strip of medium-grade sandpaper around a suitable offcut of wood and clean up the slots where necessary. The width of each slot must provide a good sliding fit for the 12mm (½in) plywood.

7 You will find it much easier to apply a finish to the components before assembling them. Clean up the panels with medium and fine sandpaper, then brush on a thin coat of lacquer or clear sealer.

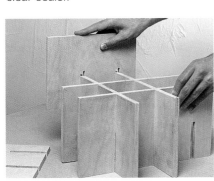

8 Slot the components together to join the rack. A dab of wood glue may be needed on the inside of each joint, but if you have finished the slots well, it should not be necessary.

PICTURE FRAME

Materials

- 1.5m (5ft) of 50 x 25mm (2 x 1in) hardwood
- 355 x 280mm (14 x 11in) of 3mm (⅛in) hardboard for the backing
- Wood glue
- Panel pins (brads)
- Retaining clips
- Fixing attachment

VISIT ANY PICTURE FRAMING SHOP and you can take your pick from literally hundreds of different frames and mouldings. There is nothing to stop you making your own, however. Some pictures will look better if displayed in a deep box frame. This one was made from white oak with a clear lacquered finish.

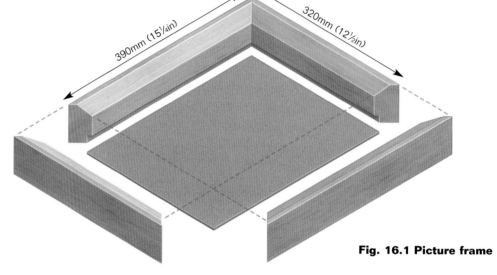

Fig. 16.1 Picture frame

390mm (15¼in)
320mm (12½in)

30°

50mm (2in)

6mm (¼in)

6mm (¼in)

25mm (1in)

Fig. 16.2 Section

Practical tip

To calculate the internal dimensions of the frame, the size of the picture should be measured off along the inner edge of the rebate (rabbet), then 6mm (¼in) subtracted from each end to determine the measurement along the inner face of the wood. Finally, add on a small margin for clearance.

Construction

This design has a chamfered profile to give the frame added depth. You can improvise any variation to suit your own taste. A section of the profile used is shown in figure 16.2. The depth of the rebate (rabbet) is determined by the thickness of glass and backing board, plus the picture and its mount.

Cut the hardboard backing to size, then have a piece of glass cut to exactly the same size. Slip the glass into place. Fit small brass clips to act as retainers for the backing and check everything for a good fit before mounting the picture.

1 Cut the four frame members roughly to length before forming the rebate. Leave them over-length at this stage. Use a plough (bullnose) or rebate plane to cut the rebate to a suitable depth in the bottom edge.

2 Turn the work over and plane a chamfer on the inner edge. Set a bevel gauge to 30 degrees, mark the angle at each end, and use a small block plane to trim accurately down to the line.

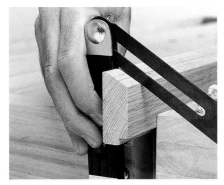

3 Check the angle of the chamfer with the bevel gauge as you work, particularly at the ends where the corners will meet.

4 Make a 45-degree mitre cut at one end of each frame member with a mitre saw. Calculate your internal measurements as instructed.

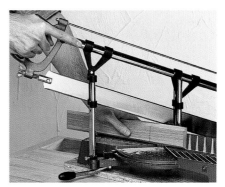

5 Mark this measurement on the inner face and square a line across the face. Align the mitre saw with this line and cut each piece to the right length.

6 Use mitre (frame) cramps to hold the assembly together while you check that the mitres are a good fit. Make any adjustments with a block plane, apply glue to each face and reassemble, tightening the clamps.

7 Fasten each corner with a couple of panel pins to lock them together. In a very hard wood such as oak, it is advisable to drill short pilot holes to avoid splitting the delicate mitre joints.

8 Before the glue has set, fit a web clamp around the frame. This helps keep the assembly square. Tighten the ratchet clamp with a spanner (wrench), check the frame with a try square and leave for the glue to dry.

9 When the glue has set, clean up the edges of the frame and sand smooth all round by hand. Apply the finish and fittings of your choice.

CD RACK

THE IDEA FOR THIS COMPACT DISC storage system came about because a piece of cherry wood, with distinctive figure in the grain, and a short offcut of waney-edged yew with an interesting shape were found in the workshop. You can use any type of wood, of course, possibly something left over from another job. With a little imagination, you can turn short lengths of wood into all manner of items.

Materials

- 760mm (30in) of 125 x 25mm (5 x 1in) hardwood for the rack
- 760mm (30in) of 25 x 12mm (1 x ½in) hardwood for the sides
- 280mm (11in) of 150 x 19mm (6 x ¾in) hardwood for the base
- Wood glue
- Brass panel pins (brads)

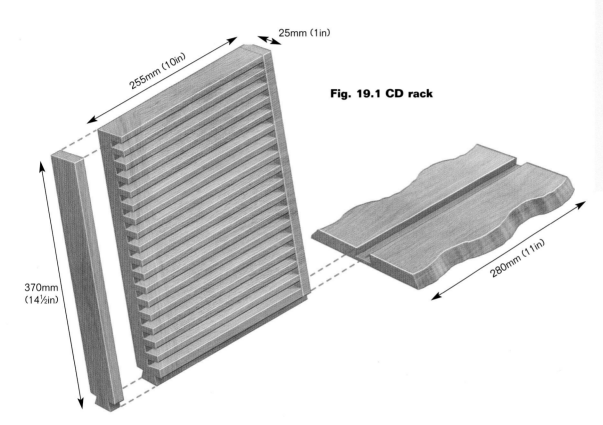

25mm (1in)

255mm (10in)

Fig. 19.1 CD rack

370mm (14½in)

280mm (11in)

Construction

The design is simplicity itself – it uses the cantilever principle to support the weight of the CDs. A width of 255mm (10in) will allow two columns to be stacked side by side. The rack can be any height you like, provided the base is wide enough to make it stable. As a guide, ensure that the top of the rack, inclined at 10 degrees, is vertically above the back edge of the base. The diagram shows how to set out the ingenious dovetailed housing joint that holds the unit together.

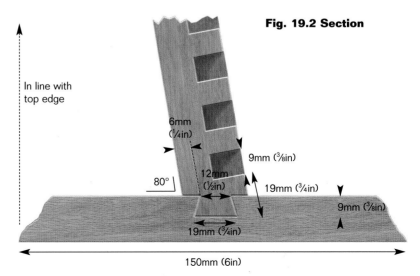

Fig. 19.2 Section

In line with top edge

6mm (¼in)

9mm (⅜in)

80°

12mm (½in)

19mm (¾in)

9mm (⅜in)

19mm (¾in)

150mm (6in)

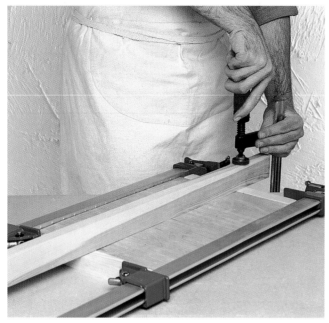

1 Cut the 125 x 25mm (5 x 1in) hardwood into two pieces 370mm (14½in) long for the main portion of the rack. Plane the edges square, glue and clamp them together. Simple butt joints are sufficient. To make sure that the board remains absolutely flat, clamp a stout batten over the top of the assembly before finally tightening the sash cramps.

2 Use a 9mm (⅜in) diameter router bit (to match the thickness of a CD cover) to rout a slot 19mm (¾in) up from the bottom edge, using the router fence as a guide. Then make a routing jig to do the rest by screwing a small strip of 9mm (⅜in) wide hardwood to the router base, exactly 9mm (⅜in) from the cutter's edge.

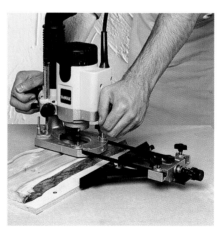

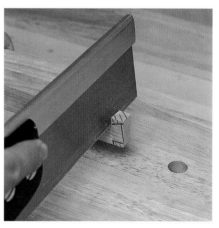

3 It is a simple matter to run the hardwood strip along each slot to position the next groove correctly. Continue in this way to the end of the board. Make sure the work is firmly clamped to the bench when doing this, or use a bench stop.

4 Use a dovetail cutter to rout the housing groove in the base. To deal with a waney edge, pin a straight-edged piece of plywood to the underside and run the router fence along it. Screw it down to the work surface so that it cannot move.

5 Cut the tails on the two side pieces with a fine dovetail saw. Use a bevel gauge to set the shoulders at an angle of 10 degrees, as shown in figure 19.2. Then make a small template to mark the shape of the tails to suit the profile of the dovetail groove.

6 Use the same template to mark out the bottom edge of the main upright. Scribe the shoulders along its length with a marking gauge, and clamp a straightedge along the shoulder line to guide the tenon saw. Keep the saw blade perfectly level to ensure the shoulders are straight and parallel.

7 To form the tail on the upright, plane the required angle on a scrap piece of wood to make an accurate guide for a small shoulder plane. Use a paring chisel to remove the waste from the corners. The angles are different on each face because of the sloping profile, and should match those on the two side pieces.

8 Plane the bottom edge of the tail to the required angle to complete the joint, paring it down until the tail has a good sliding fit in the housing. Before fitting the side pieces, you should clean up each groove with a small sanding block.

9 Pin and glue the side pieces to the upright, using small brass panel pins. Align the dovetails accurately and position the pins to avoid the slots. Apply glue to the dovetailed housing in the base and slide the rack into place. When the glue is dry, apply the desired finish.

Bookshelf

Manufactured boards with veneered faces, sometimes called decorative boards, can make quick work of any project. However, the exposed edges of veneered plywood and MDF are vulnerable to damage and not at all attractive. To overcome this drawback, you can buy ready-made solid wood trim to match most common types of veneer, or you can make your own if you have the right tools. This bookshelf was made from boards veneered with American white oak, edged with darker oak trim to provide a contrast.

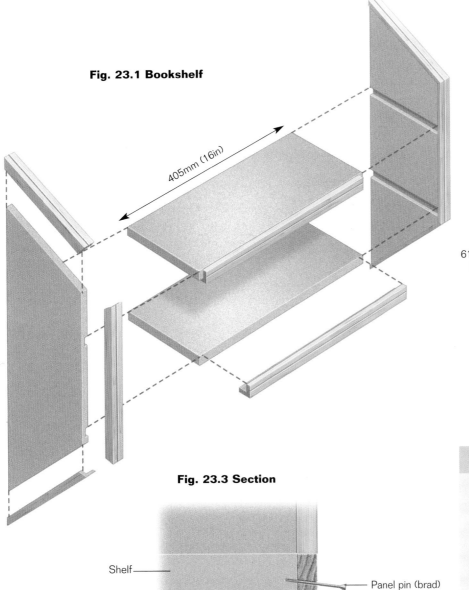

Fig. 23.1 Bookshelf

405mm (16in)

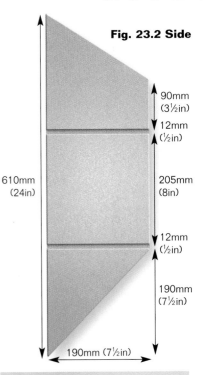

Fig. 23.2 Side

90mm (3½in)

12mm (½in)

610mm (24in)

205mm (8in)

12mm (½in)

190mm (7½in)

190mm (7½in)

Fig. 23.3 Section

Shelf

Panel pin (brad)

Moulding

Construction

The dimensions of this small shelf unit are provided as a guide only. You can alter them to suit your own books or any other items you may wish to display. A suitable height for most paperbacks is 205–255mm (8–10in). Bear in mind that 12mm (½in) boards will sag under heavy loads if you make the shelves too wide.

1 Set out the profile on one end of the unit, cut it out and use it as a pattern for the other end to ensure that they are a perfect match. Scribe the angled cuts across the grain with a sharp knife to avoid tearing the grain of the thin veneers. Cut just outside the line with a jigsaw, if you have one, or sharp crosscut panel saw.

2 Clamp the angled ends in a vice so that they are horizontal, then plane them down to the scribed lines with a block plane. Work with the grain angled away from you to avoid damaging the veneer. A block plane, with a finely set, sharp blade, is the ideal tool for working this material.

3 Form the housings for the shelves with a router, running it along a straightedge pinned to the inner face. A good way to ensure accuracy is to clamp the two ends together tightly and cut the grooves in one operation. Pin a strip of scrap wood to the board edge to prevent breakout at the end of the groove.

4 The boards can vary in thickness depending on the type of veneer. It is not always possible to match the size of board exactly to the diameter of the router cutter. If necessary, plane small rebates (rabbets) on the underside of each shelf until it fits the grooves perfectly. This also improves the strength of the glued joint.

5 Apply glue to the housings and slot the unit together. It is good practice to use the glue sparingly. Any excess will have to be removed completely to prevent discoloration of the veneer at the finishing stage. Wipe off with a slightly damp cloth, and avoid rubbing glue into the grain.

6 Sash cramps are ideal for holding the assembly steady while pinning the shelves in place. Small panel pins are sufficient for a small unit such as this. Check that all corners are square and leave to set overnight. Note the small scraps of wood used to protect the veneer.

7 Cut two lengths of angled moulding to trim the front edges of the shelves. The moulding shown has a small shadow line, or "quirk", running along its length. This is designed to help conceal the heads of the panel pins when punched down with a nail set (punch; see figure 23.3).

8 The same moulding is used to trim the end panels. Mitre the ends at the corners with a small tenon saw or adjustable mitre saw. To determine the correct angle for the mitred corners, place a short section of moulding in position and use it to mark pencil lines on the end panel, parallel to the front edges. Draw a line from the corner to the point of intersection to bisect the angle exactly. Then use this as a guide for setting an adjustable bevel gauge.

9 Apply wood glue to the front edges of the end panels and pin the mouldings in place. Notice how the minimum of glue has been used. This is to prevent any excess from being squeezed on to the veneer surface when the pins are punched in with the nail set. When the glue has dried, apply coloured stopping to each pinhole with a small spatula or modelling tool before sanding smooth all over, ready for finishing.

Mirror Frame

It is remarkable how a plain mirror can be enhanced by adding a narrow bevel around the edge of the glass. This bevel-edged frame, which is built to generous proportions out of thick material, creates an even more striking effect. It was made from solid ash, which has a strongly figured grain, and it is simply finished with a coat of clear pale polish.

Materials

- Sufficient 75 x 30mm (3 x 1⅛in) hardwood to surround the chosen mirror
- 4 25mm (1in) barrel nuts
- fixing attachment

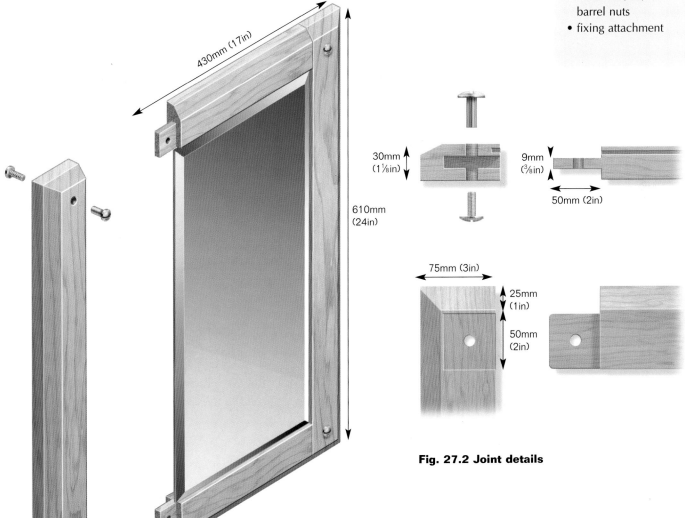

430mm (17in)

610mm (24in)

30mm (1⅛in)

9mm (⅜in)

50mm (2in)

75mm (3in)

25mm (1in)

50mm (2in)

Fig. 27.2 Joint details

Fig. 27.1 Mirror frame

Construction

The frame is made with mortise and tenon joints, and uses a clever device called a barrel nut to connect them. This is a sleeved nut, which is inserted through the cheeks of the mortise and the blade of the tenon to lock them together. Should the worst happen and the mirror have to be replaced, simply remove the bolts, tap out the barrels and the frame will come apart easily.

1 Cut the frame members to length to suit the mirror. Set out the mortise and tenons according to the dimensions given in figure 27.2. Deduct 6mm (¼in) all round from the overall size of the mirror to determine the internal size of the frame. Chop out the mortise to a depth of 50mm (2in) and clean up the corners with a bevelled chisel.

2 Cut a 25mm (1in) haunch to each tenon with a tenon saw so that the blade is 50mm (2in) square. Pare down the tenon to be a loose sliding fit in the mortise – it should not be too tight. Nip the corners off the tenon to prevent it from fouling the bottom corners of the mortise.

3 Cut a slot on the internal edge of each component to receive the mirror. The exact dimension will depend on the thickness of the mirror glass and the size of the bevelled edge. This frame required a slot only 3mm (⅛in) wide and 6mm (¼in) deep, which was carefully cut on a circular saw bench.

4 Plane a 25mm (1in) bevel on the outer edge of each frame member. The ends of the upright members, often known as stiles, will also require matching bevels. It is better to leave these until the next step, after the joint is fitted together, to achieve a good match.

5 Before assembling the frame, drill an 8mm (⁵⁄₁₆in) diameter through-hole in the centre of each mortise. Clear the waste, insert the tenon and use the same drill bit to mark the centre of the hole on the blade. While the joint is still fitted together, mark the bevel required on the ends of the stiles. Finish the corner detail with a sharp block plane.

6 Take the frame apart again to drill matching holes in the tenons. For a really perfect fit, they should be offset slightly toward the shoulder. This will draw the joint up tight when the barrel nut is inserted. Use a bradawl to offset the centre point by 1.5mm (¹⁄₁₆in). Make sure the hole is drilled straight and square.

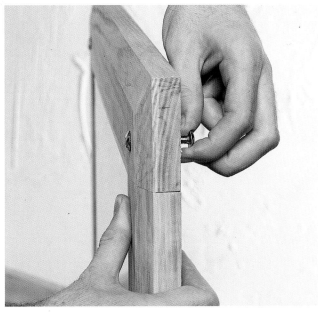

7 It is a good idea to assemble the frame first without the mirror so that you can check that everything fits perfectly. Tap two of the barrel nuts into place; you should find that the rails are drawn up tight on to their shoulders. Remove one side of the frame, slip the mirror into place and reassemble the frame.

8 Insert the male portion of the connector from the back of the frame into the threaded sleeve and tighten with a wide-bladed screwdriver. You now have a completely secure frame assembly that can be dismantled easily if you have to remove the mirror glass for any reason. Choose a suitable fixing attachment for the weight of the mirror frame.

Bar Stool

THREE DISCS OF WOOD and three lengths of round-section dowel are all it takes to make this kitchen or bar stool. The simplicity of construction is reflected in the uncluttered design, reminiscent of Shaker style. Southern yellow pine, which has a distinctive grain figure and a deep colour to the annual rings, has been used here. It has the advantage of being commonly available in wider boards, allowing each round section to be made in one piece.

Materials

- 1m (39in) of 305 x 25mm (12 x 1in) softwood for the seat and stretcher
- 2.45m (8ft) of 32mm (1¼in) diameter softwood dowel
- 6mm (¼in) plywood or MDF (medium-density fiberboard) for template
- Wood glue
- Panel pins (brads)
- 3 6mm (¼in) beech dowels

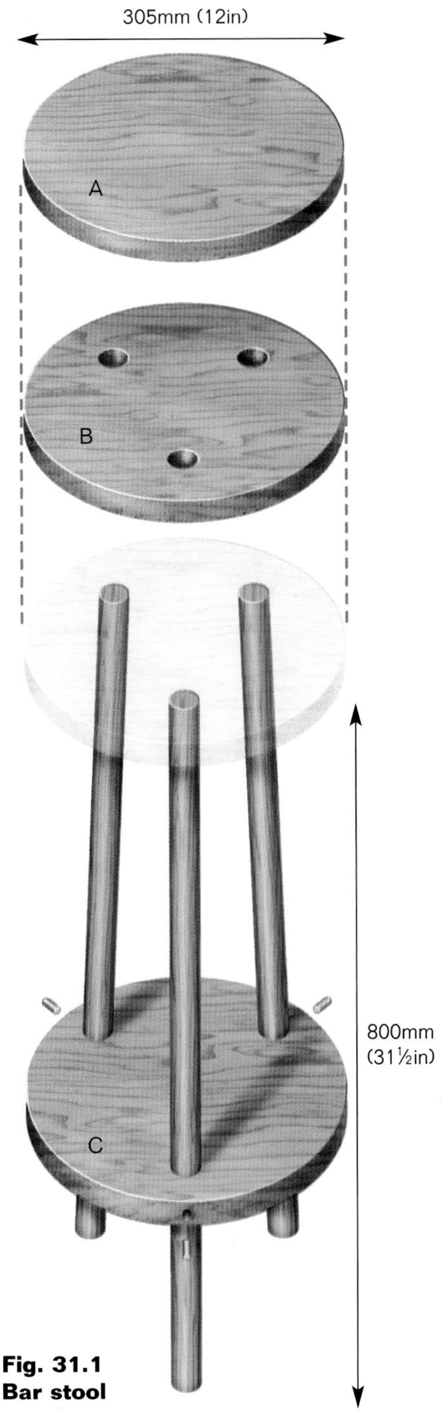

305mm (12in)

150mm (6in)

90mm (3½in)

570mm (22½in)

800mm (31½in)

125mm (5in)

230mm (9in)

**Fig. 31.1
Bar stool**

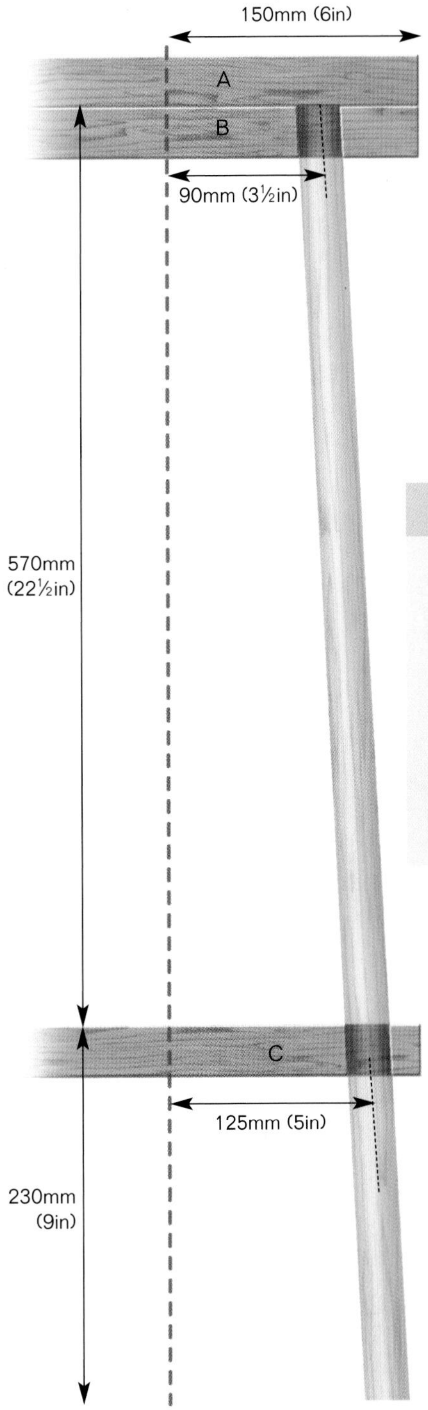

Fig. 31.2 Section

Construction

All three discs are the same diameter and are cut from one piece of board. The legs are splayed for extra stability, and instructions are given for making a jig for drilling the angled holes. Having set up to do this, you may consider making several stools at once for a matching set.

Fig. 32.1 Making a drilling jig

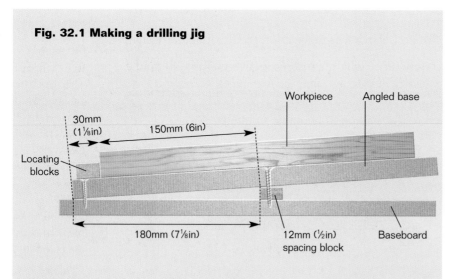

Workpiece

Angled base

30mm (1⅛in)

150mm (6in)

Locating blocks

180mm (7⅛in)

12mm (½in) spacing block

Baseboard

To drill the angled holes in the discs, make a drilling jig. First, cut a baseboard to fit under the drill stand, then screw a second board to it at an angle. You don't need to calculate the angle; simply screw a 12mm (½in) thick spacing block exactly 180mm (7⅛in) in from the front edge of the angled base. Provided you line up the centre of each disc with the centre of the jig, the holes will be set at the correct angle. Pin a couple of locating blocks to the angled base to position the disc accurately.

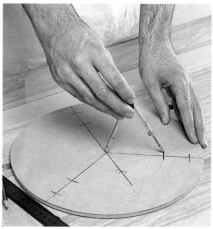

1 Make a 305mm (12in) diameter template from 6mm (¼in) MDF and draw three radial lines at 120-degree intervals to divide it into equal segments. With a pair of compasses, mark the centres of the leg positions for the top and bottom discs, and drill a small pilot hole at each point. See figure 31.2 for the dimensions required.

2 Cut three discs from the board with a jigsaw, making them oversize by about 6mm (¼in). Mark the discs A, B and C, as in the diagram. Pin the template to each piece in turn and use a template cutter fitted to the router to trim the edges to the finished size. Before removing the template from B and C, use a punch to mark the centres of the holes for the legs.

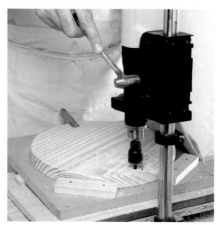

3 Fit a hole saw of the correct diameter in the drill stand and slide the drilling jig into place. Insert disc C in the jig and adjust it until the drill bit is centred exactly over one of the hole positions. Clamp the jig so that it cannot move and drill the hole. Repeat for the other two holes.

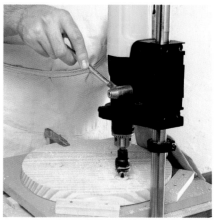

4 Drill holes in disc B in the same way – you will have to move the jig further toward the drill stand to allow for the holes being nearer the centre of the disc, but the angle remains the same.

5 Cut the legs to length and make a small wedge-shaped slot, 19mm (¾in) deep, in the top of each. Note the pencil line that identifies the outside of each leg to orient it correctly. This ensures that the angles at the bottom of the legs sit flat on the floor and keep the stool level.

6 Place disc B upside down on the workbench. Insert the legs into disc C and slide it to its position, 230mm (9in) from the ends. Before gluing, locate the tops of the legs into disc B to hold them at the correct angle. Apply glue to the holes in disc C and tap it into place, making sure that it is level. Drill a 6mm (¼in) hole into each leg and glue in a small beech dowel to secure the disc.

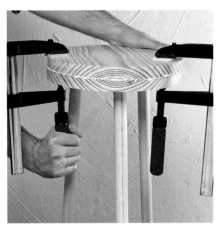

7 Leave the lower part of the assembly for the glue to dry before proceeding. When it is quite firm, carefully pull the legs away from the top disc one at a time, apply glue and tap them back into place. Keep the pencil line on each facing outward to prevent the legs from twisting out of position.

8 Turn the stool over and insert three small wedges, made from offcuts (scraps) of softwood, into the tops of the legs to lock them in place, as shown. Apply a generous amount of glue and tap the wedges firmly home. Allow the glue to dry, then plane flush with a block plane, set for a fine cut.

9 Finally, glue disc A to the top of the stool to complete the job. Two or three panel pins will prevent it from sliding around as the clamps are tightened. Note how the pattern of the growth rings has been reversed. This not only creates an attractive visual effect, but also serves to stabilize the two pieces by balancing any tendency to shrink or expand.

OCCASIONAL TABLE

No matter how fashions change, a low, neat table always makes a useful addition to the living space, and this one is a classic of its kind. With its well-proportioned, delicate frame supporting the bold, oval top, it combines clean, contemporary looks with all the best in traditional woodworking. White ash was used to make this example, and it was clear finished to bring out the honey colour of the wood.

Fig. 35.1 Occasional table

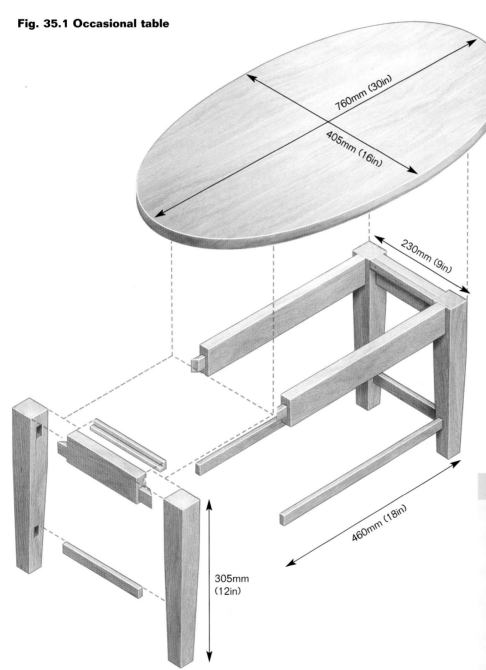

760mm (30in)

405mm (16in)

230mm (9in)

460mm (18in)

305mm (12in)

Materials

- 1.6m (63in) of 205 x 25mm (8 x 1in) hardwood for the top
- 1.25m (48in) of 38 x 38mm (1½ x 1½in) hardwood for the legs
- 1.4m (55in) of 50 x 19mm (2 x ¾in) hardwood for the top rails
- 1.4m (55in) of 25 x 12mm (1 x ½in) hardwood for the lower rails
- 6mm (¼in) MDF (medium-density fiberboard) for the template
- Wood glue
- Biscuits for jointing
- 38mm (1½in) brass wood screws
- Panel pins (brads)

Construction

The frame for this table provides a good exercise in classic carpentry, with fine detail to the tenon joints and a slight taper to the legs to add visual balance. The shape of the top was chosen, in part, to make the best of the attractive wood grain. Setting out the oval is simple with a neat geometrical device – a loop of string and two panel pins (brads).

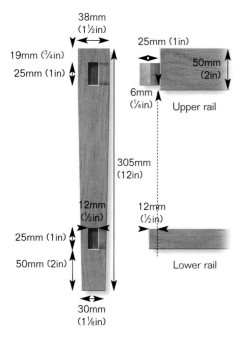

38mm
(1½in)

19mm (¾in)

25mm (1in)

25mm (1in)

50mm
(2in)

Upper rail

6mm
(¼in)

305mm
(12in)

12mm
(½in)

12mm
(½in)

25mm (1in)

50mm (2in)

Lower rail

30mm
(1⅛in)

Fig. 36.1 Leg detail

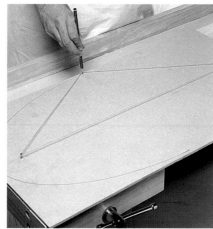

1 The size of the top determines the proportions of the frame below, so start by setting out an oval shape to suit your pieces of wood. Cut a template panel so that it is slightly larger than the overall size of the top, and insert two panel pins on the centre line as shown. A loop of string placed over the pins will allow a pencil to describe a perfect ellipse. Practise with the length of string until you achieve a profile that looks right.

2 Cut two top boards to a suitable length, plane their edges square and insert biscuits in the edges prior to gluing them together. Position the biscuits in such a way that they will not be exposed when cutting the top to its final shape. Clamp the boards with sash cramps and leave to set while you make the frame.

3 Set out the mortises for the legs by following the dimensions in the diagram. The taper begins 50mm (2in) below the top of the leg so that the shoulders of the upper rails can be cut square. Note that the mortise for each lower rail is more of a socket, being the full size of the rail itself; no shoulders are required.

4 Pare the tenons on the upper rails with a wide bevelled chisel or shoulder plane. Accuracy is vital for this assembly to ensure that all mating parts make good contact for the adhesive. Even the small shoulders at the sides of the tenons play a part in keeping the frame square and rigid.

5 The tenons intersect inside the mortise at the top of each leg. Cut a mitre on the end of each tenon and check each corner in turn so that there is a snug fit. Mark up the rails and legs in their respective positions before moving on to fashion the tapers on the legs.

6 Scribe guidelines around the foot of each leg with a marking gauge. Use a straightedge to form the outline of the taper on two opposing faces and plane carefully down to the lines. Work from the top of each leg, with the grain, down toward the tapered ends.

7 On the faces you have just planed, mark the same taper profile for the remaining two sides and repeat the operation. Note the wedge in the vice that clamps the tapered leg in position. The tapered ends should be 30mm (1⅛in) square when you have finished.

8 The two short rails are grooved to receive the rebated (rabbeted) blocks that connect the frame to the top. Use a plough (bullnose) plane to form the 9 x 9mm (⅜ x ⅜in) housing, then fashion two fixing blocks from an offcut (scrap) of 19 x 19mm (¾ x ¾in) hardwood.

9 Assemble the frame, upside-down, on a flat surface to ensure that it is square and level. Glue, cramp and leave to dry while you work on the table top. Cut out the oval shape of the template with a jigsaw and smooth the edges. Pin it to the underside of the top, and use a router with a template follower to transfer the shape.

10 Plane the table top flat, sand it smooth and, if desired, rout a profile around the edge. Drill and countersink the small fixing blocks for 38mm (1½in) brass wood screws and fix the frame to the top. There is no need to use glue – this type of attachment method allows the solid top to shrink or expand slightly without disturbing the frame assembly.

STORAGE CHEST

THIS IS A CLASSIC STORAGE CHEST with traditional lines, which can be used as a linen chest in the bedroom, or perhaps as a window seat or toy chest. The clean design, with discreet brass fittings, makes it equally suitable for contemporary and period-style interiors. The chest was made from reclaimed pine floorboards, which have a deep orange colour that is rare in new-grown softwoods. A clear wax finish brings out the full character of the grain.

Materials

- 11m (36ft) of 150 x 25mm (6 x 1in) softwood
- 6.7m (22ft) of 50 x 25mm (2 x 1in) softwood
- 915 x 380mm (36 x 15in) of 6mm (¼in) MDF (medium-density fiberboard)
- 915mm (36in) brass piano hinge
- Wood glue
- Biscuits for jointing
- 25mm (1in) panel pins (brads)
- 38mm (1½in) countersunk wood screws
- 2 brass lid stays
- 2 brass drop handles

Fig. 39.2 Section

Construction

This design relies on the gluing together of pine boards to make wide panels, the edges being butt jointed and reinforced with biscuits to align them. You will find a mitre saw invaluable for cutting all the joints for the sides and ends.

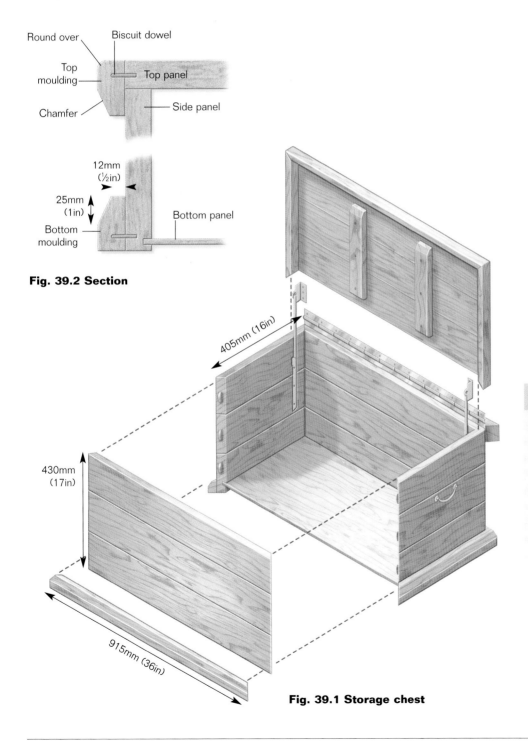

Fig. 39.1 Storage chest

1 Cut all the boards roughly to length and plane the long edges square for butt joints. Align the boards with a try square and straightedge to set out mitre cuts at each end. Make pencil marks at about 300mm (11¾in) intervals for the biscuits.

2 You may find that the mitre saw is not quite accurate enough to produce a perfect joint every time. Make a mitred shooting board, as shown, so that you can true (square) the ends of each piece with a block plane, set for a fine cut.

3 Rout a 6mm (¼in) groove in the bottom board of each panel to receive the base panel. The easiest way to clean up the groove is with a sheet of medium-grade sandpaper wrapped around a thin strip of plywood.

4 Insert biscuits and glue up each panel in turn. The biscuits will help keep the faces of the boards flush and level, as well as adding strength to the edge joint. Make sure the mitred ends are aligned perfectly, tidying them up with a block plane if necessary.

5 Use a biscuit jointer, set at 45 degrees, to cut slots in the mitred faces at the corners. Insert the biscuits and glue the box together with wood glue. Slide the bottom panel into place before putting on the last side of the box. Clamp and leave to dry.

6 Cut the material roughly to length for the top and bottom mouldings, then plane a chamfer on one face of each piece. Figure 39.2 shows the dimensions used for this chest, but you can vary them to suit your taste. Check the angle with a bevel gauge.

7 Mitre the ends of the bottom mouldings so that they fit the external dimensions of the base. Use more biscuits to hold them flush with the bottom edges. Lock each joint with 25mm (1in) panel pins.

8 Glue and clamp three boards for the lid. To make it stay flat, alternate the orientation of each board's growth rings. Cramp from above and below to equalize the pressure on the joints.

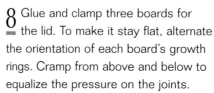

9 Form a rounded edge on the top mouldings, then mitre the corners and fit to the front and sides of the lid. Omit the back edge at this stage.

10 Sand down the top of the lid and smooth the edges. The back edge is visible, showing how the ends of the mouldings are mitred.

11 Before fitting the lid, make up two battens to fit on the underside. These stiffen the top, keep it flat and allow the chest to be used as a seat.

12 Chamfer the edges of each batten with a plane, and make matching cuts at the ends, using a dovetail or tenon saw. Glue and screw the battens to the inside of the lid. Note that they should be located at least 32mm (1¼ in) in from the back edge.

13 The final length of top moulding is fitted to the chest, not to the lid. Use a rebate (rabbet) plane to cut a shallow rebate for the brass piano hinge. It must be deep enough to accommodate the thickness of both leaves of the hinge – no more than 1.5mm (¹⁄₁₆in).

14 Mitre the ends of the moulding to fit the back of the lid, and screw it to the chest so that it projects above the top edge to match the thickness of the lid. Double check that the hinge rebate lies parallel to the edge.

15 Screw the piano hinge along the back edge of the lid, using small countersunk screws, then put the lid in place, slotting the lower hinge leaf into the rebate. Attach it with a couple of screws at each end first, then check for smooth opening and closing before adding the rest.

16 Attach the brass stays. Adjust the sliding arm of each stay so that the lid is held in a position just beyond the vertical to prevent straining the hinge. Finally, attach the drop handles to each end of the chest.

THREE-LEGGED CHAIR

THIS THREE-LEGGED CHAIR is made in a traditional Windsor fashion, the seat acting as a mounting structure for the two front legs, which are wedged and glued. The back leg is attached by a tenon so it can extend above the seat to form the back. This form of chair was common in the medieval period, although all the elements would have been turned and the seat would have been a triangle.

Materials

- 700mm (27½in) of 100 x 40mm (4 x 1½in) beech for the back leg
- 850mm (33½in) of 40 x 40mm (1½ x 1½in) beech for the front legs
- 210mm (8¼in) of 40 x 40mm (1½ x 1½in) beech for the back rest
- 2 330mm (13in) lengths of 135 x 40mm (5¼ x 1½in) beech for the seat
- 390mm (15¼in) of 60 x 40mm (2¼ x 1½in) beech for the seat
- Plywood for the template
- Wood glue
- Biscuits for jointing
- Small dowel

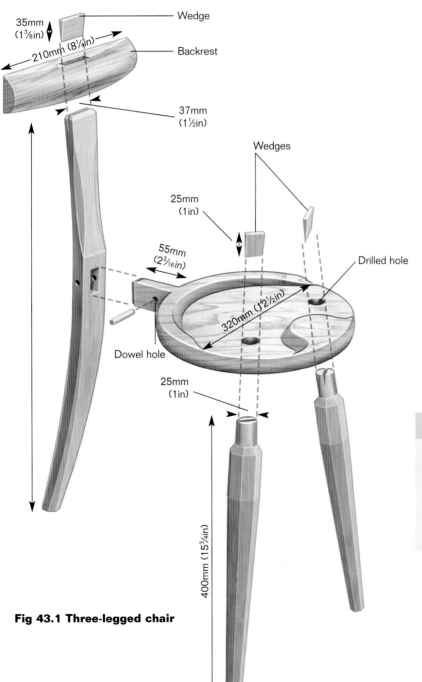

Fig 43.1 Three-legged chair

Construction

This chair relies on one of the most common joints, the mortise and tenon. Two of the joints are round and wedged, but work on the same principle as the rectangular variety.

1 The seat is formed from three pieces of wood. Plane a face side and edge on each of these boards, prior to cutting them to length. Square edges are essential for jointing the boards if the seat is to be flat.

2 Cut the prepared boards to size and form a tenon on the end of the centre section, which will fit into the mortise in the back leg. The central square strip in the seat makes cutting this joint easier.

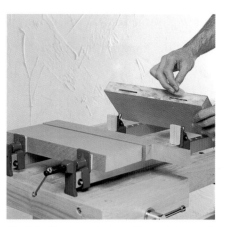

3 Join the boards together with wood glue and biscuits, using sash cramps to hold them while the glue sets. Leave to set overnight as the joint will be stronger if fully cured before removing the cramps.

4 Make a plywood template to match the profile of the back leg, then mark and cut out the leg from a planed piece of wood.

5 Cut out the seat shape with a jigsaw and drill the angled holes for the front legs. Either make a drilling jig, or cut the angle on a scrap piece of wood and stand this next to each hole position so that the drill can be held at the same angle, as shown.

6 Plane the front leg blank into a hexagonal section before cutting it in half to form the two legs. Allow enough timber for the saw cuts.

7 Plane a taper on each front leg, as shown in the diagram, working from opposing sides to form a square at the base.

8 Use a V-block to hold the leg firmly in place while you remove the corners to complete the tapered hexagonal section.

9 Make an angled cut with a tenon saw in the top of the leg to match the angle of the hole drilled in the seat. Using a chisel, form a 25mm (1in) round peg to fit the hole. Cut the mortise in the back leg to fit the seat tenon.

10 Use a spokeshave to form the chamfers on the back leg. Shape the leg in the same way as the front legs to create a tapering hexagonal section, taking care to leave the cheeks of the mortise square.

11 Having already cut the mortise in the backrest for the back leg, plane the backrest to shape, rounding off the front face. Create a taper on the back of the rest, as shown, using a block plane.

12 Using a shallow gouge, start carving out a concave shape in the seat blank.

13 Continue in this way until you are satisfied with the shape; be careful not to remove too much material around the points where the legs join. Round the edge of the seat with a spokeshave.

15 Make a saw cut into the peg at the top of each front leg, apply glue and insert the peg into its hole in the seat. Secure the leg by driving a small wooden wedge into the cut in the peg. Secure the backrest to the top of the back leg in the same way. Remove any excess material when the glue has dried.

14 Drill a small dowel hole through the back leg mortise, insert the seat tenon and mark the position of the hole on it. Remove the tenon and drill the hole slightly off-centre, toward the seat. Attach the leg using a small dowel. When the dowel is driven home, it will pull the joint together.

DISPLAY CASE

A COLLECTION OF INTERESTING OR PRECIOUS ARTEFACTS can be seen to best advantage if displayed in a purpose-made cabinet. Whatever you may want to show off, you can keep everything safe behind the sleek glass doors of this custom-built case. It is a simple pine box with a separate insert of pigeon-hole compartments, which can be removed for easy cleaning.

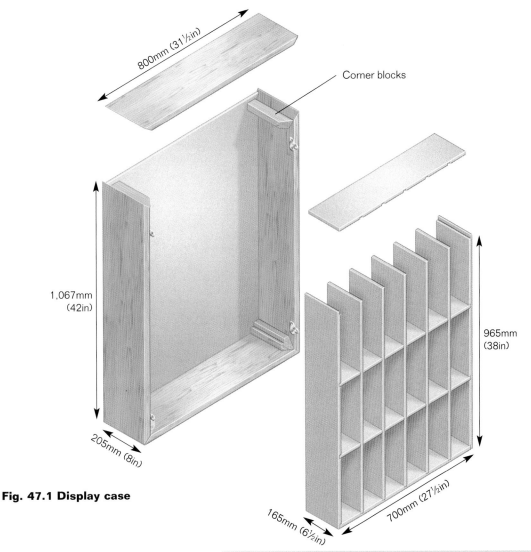

Corner blocks

800mm (31½in)

1,067mm (42in)

205mm (8in)

965mm (38in)

165mm (6½in)

700mm (27½in)

Fig. 47.1 Display case

Materials

- 3.8m (12ft 6in) of 205 x 25mm (8 x 1in) softwood
- 1m (39in) of 38 x 38mm (1½ x 1½in) softwood for the corner blocks
- 1050 x 775mm (41 x 30½in) of 6mm (¼in) MDF (medium-density fiberboard) for the back panel
- 1.65 x 1.25m (65 x 48in) of 12mm (½in) MDF for the inserts
- Glass doors cut to size
- Glass door hinges and magnetic catches
- Wood glue
- Biscuits for jointing
- 50mm (2in) countersunk wood screws
- Panel pins (brads)

Construction

The cabinet can be made to any size. This one was based on 18 compartments, each measuring 300 x 100mm (11¾ x 4in). Make a scale drawing of the ideal arrangement of compartments and calculate the external size of the box from this. There is a 25mm (1in) gap between the insert and the outer box.

Fig. 47.2 Making the insert

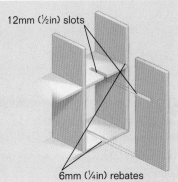

The shelf insert is made from MDF (medium-density fiberboard) then painted to provide a contrast with the natural wood finish of the cabinet. The sides, top and bottom of the insert are rebated (rabbeted) 6mm (¼in) deep to receive the inner dividers, which are slotted to interlock. The top and bottom are also rebated into the sides, making all the horizontal pieces the same length.

12mm (½in) slots

6mm (¼in) rebates

Fig. 48.1 Ordering the doors

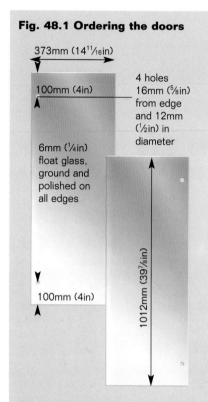

373mm (14^{11}/$_{16}$in)

100mm (4in)

4 holes 16mm (^{5}/$_8$in) from edge and 12mm (^{1}/$_2$in) in diameter

6mm (^{1}/$_4$in) float glass, ground and polished on all edges

1012mm (39^7/$_8$in)

100mm (4in)

Measure the internal dimensions of the box and calculate the size of glass required for the doors. Subtract 1.5mm (^{1}/$_{16}$in) all round for clearance and a similar amount where the doors meet in the centre. The hinges used required small holes to be drilled in the glass – definitely a job for a specialist. Take a sketch to your glazier when you order the doors.

1 Cut the four sides to length, using a powered crosscut saw to form the mitres in the softwood. This particular saw has sliding bars on the body that enable it to be extended to cut wide boards.

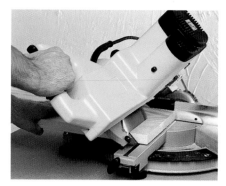

2 A mitred shooting board is used to tidy up the face of each joint to ensure perfectly square corners. The end of the shooting board must be planed to a 45-degree angle to guide the sole plate of the block plane.

3 The corner joints are aligned using biscuits. This biscuit jointer has an adjustable front fence that makes it very easy to set the required angle, a feature to look for when buying.

4 Use a router or rebate (rabbet) plane to cut 6mm (^{1}/$_4$in) deep by 12mm (^{1}/$_2$in) wide rebates along the back edges of the box to receive the recessed back panel.

5 Depending on the type of hinge being used, you may need to chisel a small recess for each hinge mounting plate. Glass door hinges are specialized items, so be sure to obtain them before you start the job.

6 Prepare four corner blocks from a length of 38 x 38mm (1^1/$_2$ x 1^1/$_2$in) batten. Cut a 12 x 12mm (^{1}/$_2$ x ^{1}/$_2$in) rebate along one edge and cut four pieces with angled ends. The overall length of each block is 150mm (6in).

7 Apply glue to the mitred ends of the boards, insert the biscuits and clamp the box together, face down on the bench. Use small offcuts (scraps) of rebated corner block to protect the corners under the cramp heads.

8 Check that the box is square, then lay the MDF back panel into its rebate. Attach it securely with panel pins. The panel will help keep the box square when you turn it over.

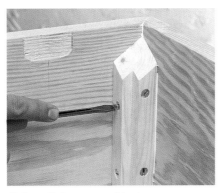

9 Install the corner blocks to ensure the box is square – vital for a good fit for the glass doors. The bevel at the front of each block guides the insert into position, making the block less apparent when the cabinet is complete.

10 To make the insert, cut the MDF into strips, 165mm (6½in) wide, then cut them to their respective lengths. Mark out all the rebates and slots on all parts, clamping them in pairs so that they match perfectly.

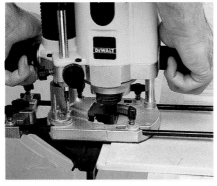

11 Set the depth stop of the router to cut 6mm (¼in) deep rebates and grooves in the outer panels. Use a fence when making the edge cuts. Clamp a straightedge to the work when forming the remaining housing joints.

12 Create the slots in the dividers by routing halfway across the width of the piece. You should square the end of each slot with a 12mm (½in) bevelled chisel.

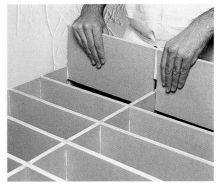

13 Assemble the box using glue and panel pins. Slide each divider into place – the construction will become quite rigid as each bit is added. Check that all is square, wipe off any excess glue with a damp cloth and leave to dry.

14 Before attaching the insert, add the hinges to match the hole positions in the glass doors. This type of hinge is best for glass doors and provides a positive fixing through glass.

15 The chrome-plated clips on the doors act as striker plates for the magnetic touch latch. This device springs the door open with a light touch, so no handles are needed.

16 Offer the insert into position to ensure that it is a good sliding fit before painting. Tap it all the way in. Remove and apply the finish of your choice before fitting the doors.

BEDSIDE CABINET

THIS SMALL CABINET is made of American white oak veneered panels with a liming wax finish to produce a smart, contemporary look. Solid wood trim and edging are easily applied to match the oak-veneered door and panels. The grain pattern of the oak is enhanced by the pale colour, while the wax finish suits the soft, comfortable feel of a bedroom.

Materials

- 1.5 x 1m (60 x 39in) of 12mm (½in) veneered MDF (medium-density fiberboard)
- 305 x 305mm (12 x 12in) of 6mm (¼in) MDF for the template
- 1.5m (60in) of 19 x 19mm (¾ x ¾in) hardwood moulding for the top
- 4m (13ft) of 12 x 6mm (½ x ¼in) hardwood edge trim
- Pre-glued veneer edging strip
- 2 brass hinges
- Ball catch
- Door handle
- 4 brass shelf supports
- Wood glue
- 19mm (¾in) panel pins (brads)
- 12mm (½in) countersunk brass wood screws

Construction

The distinctive profile of the cabinet sides incorporates a simple curve that forms the legs at the bottom and a matching handle detail at the top. Pre-glued strips of veneer simplify the process of applying edging to the shape. The top of the cabinet is finished with an angled moulding, which forms a shallow recess on the top to prevent stray items from rolling off. With a router and a few basic hand tools, this project can be constructed with ease.

Fig. 51.2 Profile

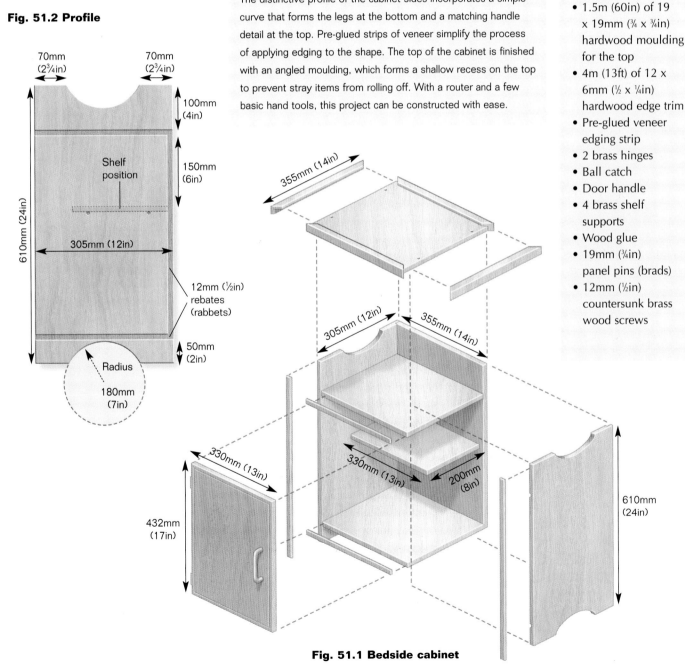

70mm (2¾in)   70mm (2¾in)

100mm (4in)

Shelf position

150mm (6in)

610mm (24in)

305mm (12in)

12mm (½in) rebates (rabbets)

50mm (2in)

Radius

180mm (7in)

355mm (14in)

305mm (12in)   355mm (14in)

330mm (13in)

330mm (13in)   200mm (8in)

432mm (17in)

610mm (24in)

Fig. 51.1 Bedside cabinet

1 Cut the two side panels to their overall size, using a router with a 12mm (½in) cutter to rebate (rabbet) them for the shelves and back panel. Set out the rebates according to the dimensions given in figure 51.2. Cut out the back panel and rebate at top and bottom for the horizontal panels.

2 Make a template using 6mm (¼in) thick MDF to the radius shown. Line up the centre line of the template with the centre of the panel and transfer the shape to each end. Remove the waste with a jigsaw, set to a slow speed to avoid forcing the blade through the work.

3 Smooth down the curves with a pad of sandpaper, taking care not to round over the edges of the cutout. The edging strip requires a perfectly flat surface when it is applied. Use a rotary sanding drum if you have one.

4 Using the tip of a warm iron, press the pre-glued strip into place so that it follows the curve. Keep the iron moving at all times to avoid overheating the delicate material. Leave for at least 15 minutes for the glue to set.

5 Trim off the excess veneer with a long, flat blade, pressed flat on the surface of the panel. This helps to prevent splinters from being picked up by the blade. Use a slow knifing action in long strokes to remove the small slivers of veneer.

6 Drill four small holes, 6mm (¼in) deep, for the support pegs of the removable shelf before assembling the cabinet. Note the masking tape on the drill bit, which acts as a depth gauge. Then sand down all the internal surfaces.

7 Assemble the cabinet face down on a flat surface. Apply glue to the rebates and slot in the horizontal panels. Push the back panel firmly into position to square the assembly.

8 Use 19mm (¾in) panel pins to attach the joints. Check the cabinet is square and that all front edges are flush. Wipe off excess glue with a damp cloth and allow to dry.

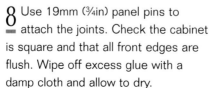

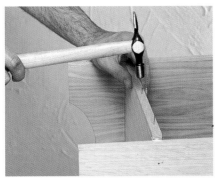

9 Cut short lengths of 6mm (¼in) hardwood edge trim to fit the front edges of the horizontal panels. Glue and pin them in place, taking care not to position the pins too close to the ends to prevent the material from splitting. A small pilot hole may be required for each pin.

10 Mitre four pieces of moulding to edge the top panel. Fit the front and back sections of moulding to the panel, gluing and pinning them as for the front trim. Centre the top on the cabinet and attach, using four narrow-gauge screws; they will be hidden by the remaining lengths of moulding.

11 Glue and pin the two side mouldings in position. Punch down all the heads, apply stopping to the pin holes and sand down ready for finishing. Take care when sanding veneered edges. Use a hand sanding block rather than a power sander.

12 Measure up and cut the door to size from a matching panel of veneered board, making it just over 6mm (¼in) smaller all round to allow for the edge trim. Mitre the ends of the trim pieces and glue them in place, then sand to a fine finish.

13 Flush hinges of the type shown require no recesses for the leaves. The barrel of the hinge pin lodges against the front edge of the side panel and automatically aligns the door. Fit with 12mm (½in) countersunk brass screws.

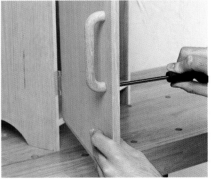

14 Screw the wooden handle of your choice to the door before fitting the catch. This allows you to control the closing action more easily and avoid straining the hinges. Now fit the brass ball catch just behind the handle.

15 A quick and easy way to align the tip of the ball catch is to apply a dab of ink to the base, and close the door on to it to make a small mark.

16 Make the removable shelf. Finish the front edge with a length of edging strip. Insert the shelf supports and offer the shelf into position. Coat the cabinet inside with clear lacquer.

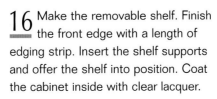

BUTCHER'S BLOCK

NO WELL-EQUIPPED KITCHEN would be complete without a good, solid butcher's block to provide a self-contained workstation for chopping and preparing ingredients. Here, laminating is used to make the chopping block from solid, hardwearing maple. This project incorporates the worktop into a sturdy freestanding table unit. It includes an optional drawer for your chopping and cutting utensils.

Construction

The table legs are made from large-section timber (lumber), and the rails are equally sturdy, being tenoned into the legs to provide a strong support for the chopping surface. This assembly has a painted finish and a coat of hardwearing clear lacquer for hygiene and durability. The knots were treated with a shellac sealer so that they would cause no problems in the finished table.

Materials

- 3.6m (12ft) of 75 x 75mm (3 x 3in) softwood for the legs
- 3.7m (12ft 2in) of 75 x 38mm (3 x 1½in) softwood for the rails
- 2m (6ft 6in) of 75 x 12mm (3 x ½in) tongued-and-grooved cladding boards for the shelf
- 1.6m (63in) of 19 x 19mm (¾ x ¾in) softwood for the shelf battens
- 2.4m (8ft) of 25 x 12mm (1 x ½in) softwood for the drawer runners
- 400mm (15¾in) of 125 x 19mm (5 x ¾in) softwood for the drawer front
- 400 x 400mm (15¾ x 15¾in) of 12mm (½in) plywood for the drawer sides
- 400 x 400mm (15¾ x 15¾in) of 6mm (½in) plywood for the drawer bottom
- 7.3m (24ft) of 50 x 35mm (2 x 1⅜in) hardwood for the top
- Wood glue
- 38mm (1½in) lost-head nails
- 6mm (¼in) dowels
- 38mm (1½in) countersunk wood screws
- 25mm (1in) round-head wood screws
- 4 metal corner brackets
- Drawer handle

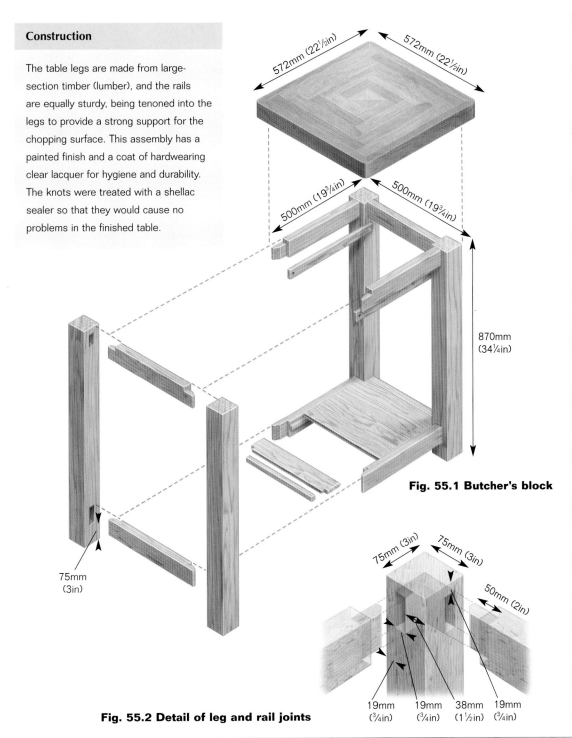

Fig. 55.1 Butcher's block

Fig. 55.2 Detail of leg and rail joints

Construction

The drawer is simply butt-jointed together with dowels to strengthen the corners. Apply glue to the dowels and insert them into the drawer sides. Slide the bottom panel into place and tap the assembly together. Clamp the corners and leave to dry, after which the front panel can be glued and screwed to the carcass.

Fig. 56.1 Drawer

325mm (12¾in)

405mm (16in)

90mm (3½in)

12mm (½in)

350mm (13¾in)

125mm (5in)

1 To make the body of the block, cut the legs to length and make sure that their ends are absolutely square for a stable structure. Set out the mortises for the rails according to the dimensions in the accompanying diagram. Clamp the legs together in pairs to allow accurate marking out. Note that the mortises for the top rails are set back from the top edges, or "relished" (revealed), by 19mm (¾in).

2 Cut the mortises, cleaning out the corners with a bevelled chisel. The tenons of each adjacent pair of rails meet in the centre of the leg, at the bottom of the blind mortises, so make sure that they are deep enough and that all the waste is removed.

3 The tenons are "bare-faced" in that the shoulder is formed on only one side of the tenon. This has the effect of moving the inner face of the rail inward while centralizing the mortise in the leg for maximum strength.

4 Mitre the ends of the tenons where they will intersect, paring them down until they both fit together perfectly inside each corner joint. This allows longer tenons and provides a stronger glue bond. The lower rails are treated in the same way, but as they are located 75mm (3in) from the ends of the legs, no "relish" is required.

5 Begin assembling the components by gluing and clamping the legs and rails together in pairs. Set up two sash cramps (clamps) on the workbench to tighten the joints of each sub-assembly. Note the small offcuts (scraps) of wood that protect the soft timber from bruising under the cramp heads.

6 Complete the construction with the legs inverted on a flat surface to keep the unit square. Slide the two leg assemblies on to the remaining rails, remembering to glue the mating surfaces of the mitred tenons where they meet inside each leg.

7 Apply sash cramps and lock the tenons in place with 38mm (1½in) lost-head nails at the inner corners of the legs. Punch the nail heads just below the surface. Check that the assembly is square, wipe off excess glue and allow to dry overnight.

8 Cut four shelf support battens from 19 x 19mm (¾ x ¾in) softwood and screw them to the lower rails as shown. Set them down from the top of the rails by the thickness of the shelf and clamp in place while attaching.

9 Cut the shelf material to size from 75 x 12mm (3 x ½in) tongued-and-grooved cladding boards. You will need to plane down the end boards to achieve the correct width for the shelf. Making it in boards allows you to fit each side in turn and cut notches to clear the legs.

10 Assemble the shelf. The boards can be sprung into place by fitting the last tongue into its groove and pushing firmly downward. The result is a perfectly fitting, strong assembly with no gaps.

11 If you want to make the optional drawer, refer to the diagram for details of its construction. Cut four lengths of 12mm (½in) plywood, 90mm (3½in) wide, for the drawer ends and sides. Then use a router with a 6mm (¼in) bit to groove them for the bottom panel. Fit centre-points to mark the ends for the dowel joints.

12 Screw the bearers for the drawer runners to the legs, using a small spacing block to position them. For 25 x 12mm (1 x ½in) runners, you should leave a gap of about 30mm (1⅛in). Drill the correct size clearance holes for the screws, countersinking the heads, to prevent the ends of the runners from splitting.

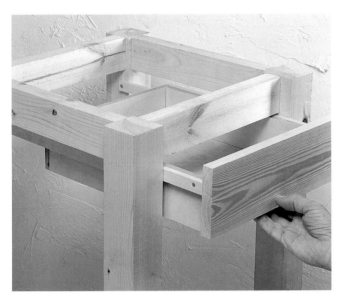

13 Finish assembling the drawer, then fit the top runners to it, flush with the top edges of the drawer tray, and offer it up to the frame to check for smooth operation. Then add the lower runners – these should be 25mm (1in) apart. The assembly is now ready for sanding and painting with the finish of your choice. Finally attach a handle to the drawer front.

14 The top of the block is made by laminating small pieces of maple together to make a herringbone pattern. All the components were prepared from quarter-sawn stock, the growth rings running vertically to the face of the block. To maintain the geometry of the design, the external size is determined by the building jig, made from straight lengths of maple screwed to a baseboard. Make sure the corners are perfectly square.

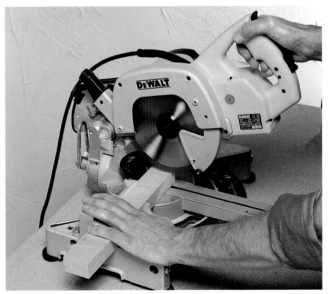

15 To make the joints as accurate as possible, each piece is fitted individually before laminating. Cut the first piece slightly oversize and use a small offcut to mark its exact length. The blocks are simply butt-jointed, so accuracy is essential. Each piece should be a sliding fit in the jig.

16 A powered crosscut saw, is a quick means of cutting accurate square ends on each component. This machine can remove the smallest sliver of wood, so cut outside the line initially and slide the work fractionally toward the blade to make a second, or even third, cut at the exact length.

17 Continue working around the jig in a clockwise direction, numbering each piece to avoid confusion later when you start to laminate the blocks into position. Working from the outside toward the centre in this way ensures that no cumulative discrepancies occur in the overall size of the block and keeps it all square.

18 The centre of the block is formed by four triangular pieces. Mark the mitres with a mitre square and a sharp scribing knife for accuracy. The final central piece should be a really tight fit to lock everything together.

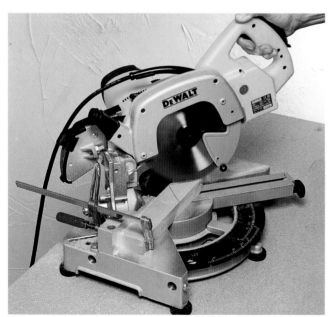

19 Making a mitre cut on a small length of wood will be safer if it is clamped firmly to the saw table. Make the first cut, swing the saw body through 90 degrees, slide the wood along to align it, then clamp it in position and make the second cut.

20 With all the components now fitted and numbered, start laminating, again from the outside toward the centre. Apply a thin film of glue to each piece and assemble the block, making sure that each piece is put into its correct place.

21 Tap the final piece of wood into position and wipe the excess glue from the surface with a damp cloth. If any hairline gaps remain, work some more glue into them and give the piece a final wipe.

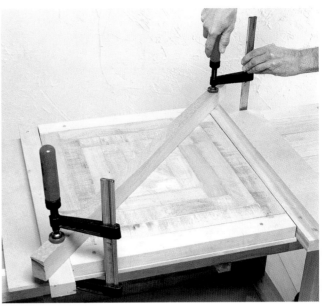

22 Tap the individual blocks firmly on to the baseboard and clamp a stout, straight-edged batten over the assembly to keep it flat as it dries. It is important to make sure the workbench underneath the board is also completely flat.

23 After at least 12 hours, remove the board from the jig and sand it down. Maple is so hard that a belt sander will probably be needed to create a flush surface, followed by a small orbital sander for a fine, smooth finish.

24 Place the top of the laminated block face-down on the workbench, align and position the leg assembly and attach the top with the corner brackets and round-head wood screws to create a sturdy fixing.

BOOKCASE

THIS BOOKCASE HAS A TOUCH OF THE CLASSICAL. With its solid proportions, clean-cut mouldings and fluted columns, it will make a stylish addition to any room in the home. The basic carcass is a straightforward box made of veneered MDF, with solid wood trim providing the extra detail. The example shown here was made from American cherry wood, left in its natural colour for the interior, but stained and polished on the outside to bring out the deep, rich figure of the grain.

Construction

The versatility of a router comes into its own for mounting the bookcase strip and fashioning the columns and mouldings, as well as making quick work of the carcass. The three types of router cutter illustrated below were used for this example, but you can vary the style of decorative detail.

Fig. 63.2 Router cutters

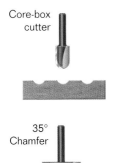

Core-box cutter

35° Chamfer

Stepped cutter

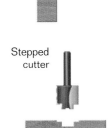

Materials

- 2.45 x 1m (8 x 3ft) of 12mm (½in) veneered MDF (medium-density fiberboard) for the carcass
- 1250 x 250mm (48 x 10in) of 25mm (1in) veneered MDF for the shelves
- 2.1m (7ft) of 100 x 25mm (4 x 1in) hardwood for the plinth
- 2.1m (7ft) of 50 x 19mm (2 x ¾in) hardwood for the bottom mouldings
- 2.1m (7ft) of 25 x 25mm (1 x 1in) hardwood for the top mouldings
- 1.8m (6ft) of 75 x 25mm (3 x 1in) hardwood for the columns
- 1.8m (6ft) of 19 x 19mm (¾ x ¾in) hardwood for the battens
- 1.2m (4ft) of 25 x 10mm (1 x ⅜in) hardwood for the shelf trim
- 2.45m (8ft) of brass bookcase strip and shelf clips
- Small countersunk brass screws
- Biscuits for jointing
- Wood glue

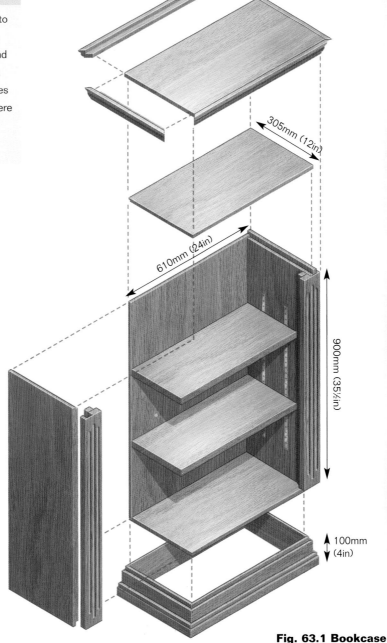

305mm (12in)

610mm (24in)

900mm (35½in)

100mm (4in)

Fig. 63.1 Bookcase

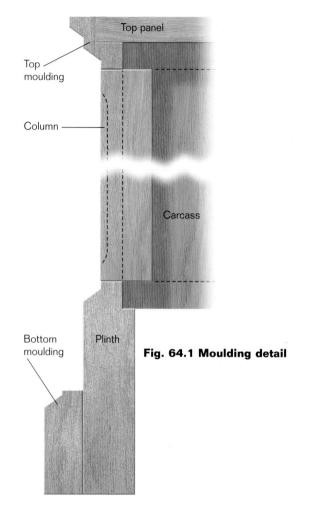

Top panel

Top moulding

Column

Carcass

Bottom moulding

Plinth

Fig. 64.1 Moulding detail

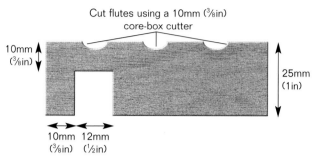

Cut flutes using a 10mm (³⁄₈in) core-box cutter

10mm (³⁄₈in)

25mm (1in)

10mm (³⁄₈in)   12mm (¹⁄₂in)

Fig. 64.2 Column detail

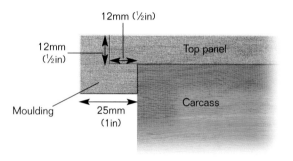

12mm (¹⁄₂in)

12mm (¹⁄₂in)

Top panel

Moulding

Carcass

25mm (1in)

Fig. 64.3 Top moulding detail

1 The carcass for the bookcase is easily made. Cut the main components to size from the sheet of veneered MDF, and form edge rebates (rabbets) in the two sides to receive the ends and back panel. Clean them up with a sanding block, taking care not to damage the delicate veneer facing.

2 Before assembling the box, the recessed bookcase strips should be fitted to the sides. Cut the brass strip into four lengths, making sure that the slots for the shelf clips will align correctly. If the strips are not identical, the shelves will not sit level. The best course is to cut one strip to size and use it as a pattern for the others.

3 Mark out the positions of the strips on each side with a carpenter's pencil, using a try square to locate them. For maximum stability, each strip should be set back from the edge of the shelf by approximately 38mm (1½in). The strips do not need to continue to the full height of the bookcase, unless you want a very shallow top shelf.

4 Rout the grooves for the inset strips, squaring the ends with a bevelled chisel. Two grooves are required for each strip – one should be equal in width to the strip itself, and another slightly deeper and wide enough to provide clearance for the hooks of the shelf clips. You can do this with two separate cutters, or invest in a special stepped cutter (shown in figure 63.2), which completes the operation in one pass.

5 It is a good idea to sand down the inner surfaces of all the panels at this stage, so that they are ready for finishing. Then fit the brass strips, using small countersunk brass screws. Make sure the slots are correctly aligned, and that the top end of each strip is fitted toward the top of the bookcase.

6 Glue and screw the carcass together, checking that it is square. Make sure that the screw heads are countersunk well below the surface. The design of the unit ensures that the screws along the edges will be concealed by the top and bottom mouldings. Leave to dry.

7 Cut four lengths of 100 x 25mm (4 x 1in) hardwood for the plinth and form a 12mm (½in) wide by 6mm (¼in) deep rebate along one edge of each to receive the bottom of the bookcase carcass. Mitre the ends and insert biscuits to reinforce and aid the alignment of the joints.

8 Glue the plinth together, strengthening the corners by adding small glued blocks. Wipe away any excess glue. Note that the internal dimensions of the rebate around the inner edge of the plinth should match the external size of the cabinet, which simply slots into position.

9 Fit the plinth over the bottom of the cabinet and secure it with small wooden blocks and screws. There is no need to glue them, as the plinth will be removed later to add the decorative moulding before sanding and finishing. It needs to be fitted at this stage to assist in aligning the fluted columns.

10 Make the columns according to the dimensions given in the diagram. Cut a 12mm (½in) housing in the back to locate each column on the front edge of the carcass, and use a core-box cutter to add the fluting to the front face (see figure 63.2). Use a small cylinder of sandpaper to remove any marks left by the cutter in the rounded flutes.

11 Screw a 19mm (¾in) batten flush with the inner edge of the housing of each column to provide a secure attachment to the carcass without any visible fixings.

12 Apply glue to the front edges of the bookcase and tap the columns into place. They should fit exactly between the top and bottom of the carcass, stiffening the sides and giving a solid, well-proportioned appearance to the whole assembly.

13 Cut the panel for the top of the bookcase and glue on the edge profile. The latter is made from 25 x 25mm (1 x 1in) stock, rebated to suit the panel, as in figure 64.3. Mitre the ends and clamp around the edges, making sure that it is perfectly flush with the surface of the panel for a smooth finish.

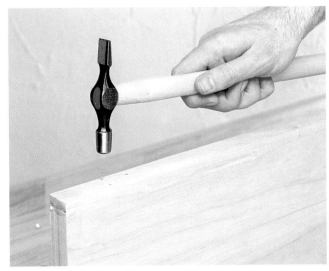

14 Check that the top panel is a good fit over the carcass – note how it locates over the top edges of the box, concealing the screws along the sides. Now you can add the moulding detail around the edges. Profile the top moulding using a 35-degree chamfer cutter (see figure 63.2). Sand, stain and polish the top and mouldings before finally attaching it to the carcass with screws from the inside. Use the same chamfer cutter to profile the plinth and bottom moulding.

15 Make two shelves for the unit, using 25mm (1in) board for extra strength. They should be slightly shorter than the internal width of the cabinet by about 1.5mm (1/16in), which will allow enough clearance for them to be tilted sideways for fitting. Glue and pin small strips of hardwood along the front edges to finish them off neatly.

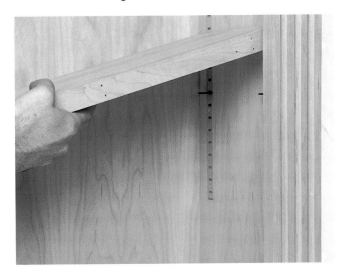

16 Insert the shelf clips into the recessed brass strips and fit the shelves.

Practical tip

To avoid having to buy a small quantity of 25mm (1in) veneered board, you can use offcuts (scraps) from the sheet of 12mm (½in) material and laminate them together.

CORNER CABINET

This elegant corner cabinet, with its limed beech finish and patterned glass doors, would make an attractive feature in the bathroom. Of relatively small dimensions, it uses literally every corner of space to provide a versatile storage unit. The front of the cabinet projects only a small amount from the wall to break up the visual line of the corner.

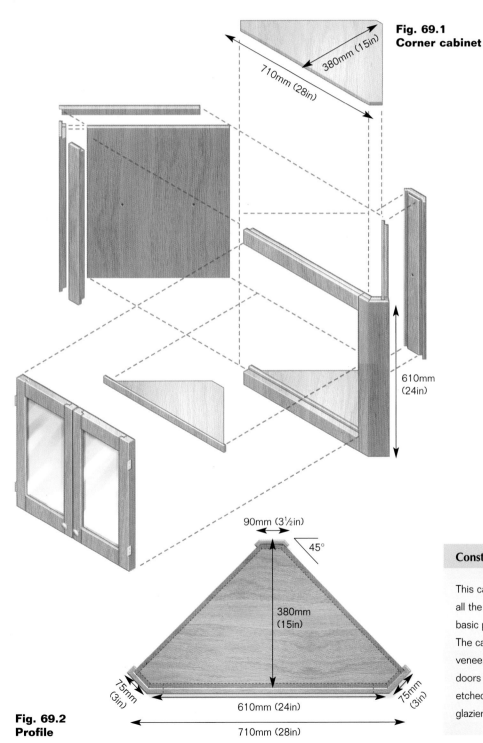

Fig. 69.1
Corner cabinet

380mm (15in)

710mm (28in)

610mm (24in)

90mm (3½in)

45°

380mm (15in)

75mm (3in)

610mm (24in)

75mm (3in)

710mm (28in)

Fig. 69.2
Profile

Materials

All materials are hardwood, unless specified otherwise:
- 1.25m (48in) of 75 x 25mm (3 x 1in)
- 3.3m (10ft 10in) of 38 x 25mm (1½ x 1in)
- 2.45m (8ft) of 50 x 25mm (2 x 1in)
- 1.25m (48in) of 50 x 10mm (2 x ⅜in)
- 610mm (24in) of 90 x 25mm (3½ x 1in)
- 3m (10ft) of 12 x 12mm (½ x ½in) glazing bead
- 1.25 x 1.25m (48 x 48in) of 12mm (½in) veneered MDF (medium-density fiberboard)
- Biscuits for jointing
- Wood glue
- 25mm (1in) and 38mm (1½in) wood screws
- 25mm (1in) panel pins (brads)
- Patterned glass for glazed doors
- Shelf supports
- 4 brass hinges
- 2 magnetic catches
- 2 door knobs

Construction

This cabinet is not as complex as it may appear – all the upright components are fitted around the basic profile, which determines the final shape. The carcass is made from 12mm (½in) ash-veneered MDF and solid beech was used for the doors and main frame members. Engraved or etched glass for the doors is available from most glaziers, who will cut it to size.

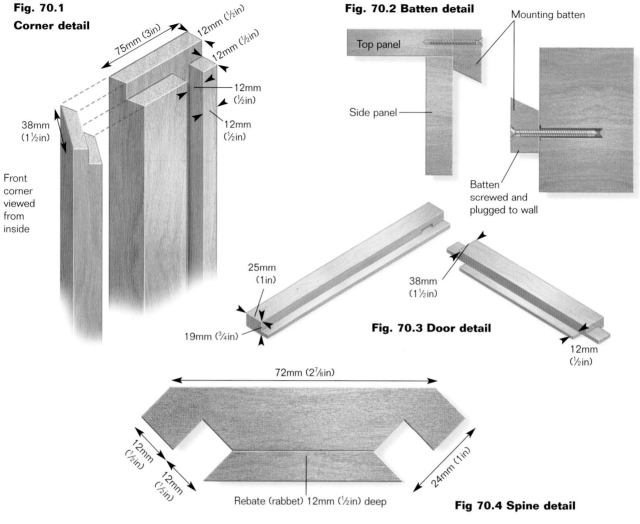

Fig. 70.1
Corner detail

75mm (3in)

12mm (½in)

12mm (½in)

12mm (½in)

38mm (1½in)

12mm (½in)

Front corner viewed from inside

Fig. 70.2 Batten detail

Mounting batten

Top panel

Side panel

Batten screwed and plugged to wall

25mm (1in)

19mm (¾in)

38mm (1½in)

Fig. 70.3 Door detail

12mm (½in)

72mm (2⅞in)

12mm (½in)

12mm (½in)

24mm (1in)

Rebate (rabbet) 12mm (½in) deep

Fig 70.4 Spine detail

1 Make a template for the basic profile, using the pattern shown in figure 69.2. The top and bottom panels, which determine the shape, are 12mm (½in) smaller all round than the external dimensions of the cabinet. Pin the template to the veneered board and cut out both panels with a jigsaw, making them slightly oversize.

2 Use a router fitted with a template cutter to finish the shape of the top and bottom panels. For the best visual effect, the grain direction of the veneer should run from side to side across the cabinet. The small pin-holes can be filled later with light-coloured wood stopping (wood filler).

3 Cut all the vertical members to the same overall length, and plane the edges of the front pieces of wood to an angle of 67.5 degrees from the outside face. When joined, these form the required internal angle of 135 degrees at the front corners.

4 All the vertical members need rebates (rabbets) at the ends for the top and bottom panels. In addition, rout 12mm (½in) housing grooves in the outer corner pieces to receive the side panels. Figure 70.1 provides a clear view of the corner detail.

5 Join the angled faces of the corner members together with biscuits. Set the angled fence of the biscuit jointer to 67.5 degrees. The biscuits not only strengthen the glued joints, but also serve to align the front edges and prevent the components from sliding apart when clamped together during the gluing process.

6 Use the bottom panel of the cabinet as a template for assembling the corner joint. Apply glue, insert the biscuits and slide the two parts together. Note how the housing groove for the side panel is aligned with the outside edge.

7 Cut the cross rails to fit between the corner uprights, rebate them to fit over the top and bottom panels and glue in place. Each is locked in position with a strip of 10mm (⅜in) hardwood that also acts as a stop for the doors. It keeps the front of the cabinet square, too.

8 Insert a side panel into the groove in one corner post, and align the top and bottom panels with a couple of 25mm (1in) panel pins. If you keep the edges flush, the cabinet will automatically conform to the desired shape as it is assembled.

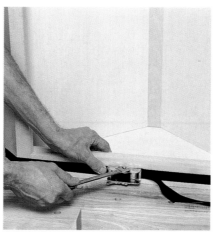

9 The rear spine member locks the side panels together and stiffens the whole structure. Cut its housing grooves according to the dimensions given in figure 70.4. Rebate the top and bottom, and slot into position. Add the second side by sliding it into place in its housing grooves in the front and back members.

10 With the second side panel in place, apply tension to the whole assembly with a pair of web cramps. These will tighten all the joints and pull the cabinet into shape. Insert more panel pins to hold the top and bottom panels in position. Check that the front is square and leave the cramps in tension as the glue dries.

11 Add short battens to the top and bottom edges of the side panels. Notch the ends of the battens to clear the corner posts, as shown, and, if wished, plane bevels on the upper pair to make a neat system for mounting the cabinet. Figure 70.2 shows how the cabinet can be simply lifted into place and hooked on to a matching pair of battens screwed to the wall.

12 Use what remains of the veneered material to make a triangular shelf for the cabinet. Set it back by 50mm (2in) from the front frame, which will allow it to be tilted and offered into position. Glue and pin a strip of wood along the front of the shelf to trim the edge.

13 To make the doors, use 38mm (1½in) stock for the stiles, and 50mm (2in) for the horizontal rails. Set out and cut the 25 x 10mm (1 x ⅜in) mortises as shown, then form 19mm (¾in) deep by 12mm (½in) wide rebates in the rear faces for the glass and beads.

14 Cut the matching tenons and rebate the rails in the same way. Note that the 25mm (1in) tenons have unequal stepped shoulders to accommodate the rebates in the stiles. Pare down to fit with a bevelled chisel. See figure 70.3.

15 Glue and assemble the two doors, clamping them together flat on the bench. The joints are so small that no wedges should be required to secure the tenons if they are a good fit. When the glue has dried, remove the projecting horns with a small tenon saw.

16 Measure the size of glass required for the doors and order the two panes from your local supplier. If using decorative etched glass, be sure to mention that they must be a matched pair with symmetrical patterns. Cut the glazing bead into lengths to hold the glass in place, but hang and fit the doors before inserting the glass.

17 Mount the brass hinges on the doors, in line with the inner edges of the rails. The offset pins make it easy to locate the hinges accurately.

Practical tip

White liming wax accentuates the delicate flecked figure of the beech wood, preserves its pale colour and protects it from the humid conditions of a bathroom.

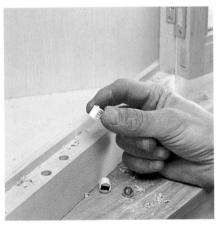

18 These miniature magnetic catches are very discreet and ideal for lightweight doors of this type. Each magnetic barrel is simply inserted into a hole drilled in the bottom rail of the frame. The small striking plate is tapped into position in the end of the door stile.

19 Finally, add two matching knobs to the doors. Sand down and apply a coat of sealer, then liming wax or your chosen finish, before fitting the glass into the doors. Fit the glazing beads using small panel pins, taking care to protect the glass as you do so.

DINING TABLE

A COMPACT DINING TABLE of striking appearance, this unique design is a composition of great subtlety and balance. The top displays the rustic quality of elm, with its swirling grain pattern and tight knot clusters. The supporting framework is made of straight-grained teak. Clear carnauba wax is the only finish required to bring out the character of the wood.

Materials

- 4.6m (15ft) of 230 x 25mm (9 x 1in) hardwood for the top
- 3m (10ft) of 75 x 75mm (3 x 3in) hardwood for the legs
- 2.1m (7ft) of 75 x 25mm (3 x 1in) hardwood for the rails
- 4m (13ft) of 50 x 25mm (2 x 1in) hardwood for the top frame
- Wood glue

690mm (27in)

1.27m (50in)

538mm (21in)

Construction

The pieces for the table top are cut from two elm boards, one of lighter tone than the other, and laminated together. The legs are tenoned through the table top to make a bold geometrical pattern.

250mm (10in)

750mm (29½in)

Practical tip

Teak may not be readily available, ecologically desirable, nor affordable, in which case you could substitute a different type of wood of contrasting colour – dark oak, for example, makes a natural partner for elm. The beauty of the design is derived from the combination of the two species. Even the wedges for the tenons use the same contrast to highlight the effect.

1.07m (42in)

Fig. 75.1 Dining table

Fig. 76.1 Top detail

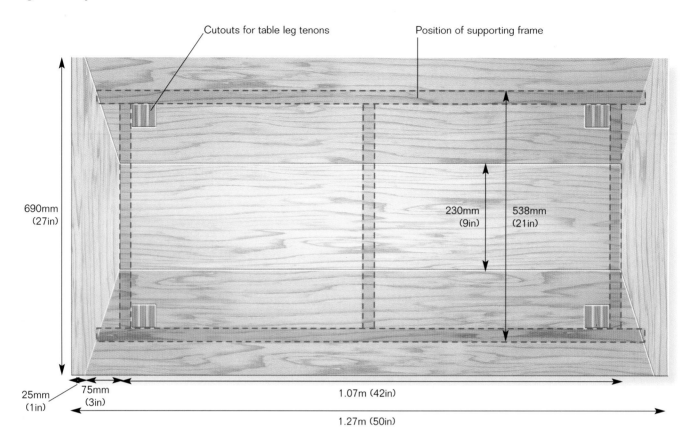

Cutouts for table leg tenons

Position of supporting frame

690mm
(27in)

230mm
(9in)

538mm
(21in)

25mm
(1in)

75mm
(3in)

1.07m (42in)

1.27m (50in)

1 The "fishtail" design of the table top is not only attractive, but also serves to lock the ends of the boards together and keep the top flat. The five components are edge-jointed, using loose tongues made of 6mm (¼in) hardwood offcuts (scraps). Cut the three main boards to the sizes shown in figure 76.1 above.

2 It is best to laminate the top in two separate stages. First glue and clamp the three long boards together, making sure that the angled ends are aligned correctly. Use two straight-edged battens to clamp the assembly flat on the bench while the glue dries.

3 Make an angled template as an aid to shaping the end sections. Pare down the edges if necessary to accommodate any discrepancy in the assembly. Position the template so that the most suitable and attractive portions of wood will be used to complete the table top. Mark out the end pieces and cut them to size.

4 Plane the edges of the end pieces so that they are absolutely square, and pare them down carefully to fit the table top. When they fit perfectly, rout the 6mm (¼in) grooves for the loose tongues. Stop the grooves short of the ends by 25mm (1in).

5 Apply glue, insert the hardwood tongues in the grooves and clamp the ends in place. Note how the grooves stop short of the ends to avoid weakening the corners. Set the top aside for the glue to dry while you work on the table frame and legs. Use weights or cramps to keep it as flat as possible.

6 Make the legs in pairs to suit each end of the table. Clamp each pair together, as shown, and set out the mortises for the lower rails. The mortises are sized at 68 x 19mm (2¾ x ¾in). This is slightly smaller than the rails, leaving a 3mm (⅛in) shoulder around each tenon.

7 At the outer face of each table leg, angle the sides of the mortise to receive the locking wedges. As the wedges have a decorative aspect, they can be generous in size, adding 6mm (¼in) to each end of the mortise.

8 Pare the tenons down to a good fit and dry-assemble the legs, making sure that the shoulders sit squarely. Then set out the mortises for the horizontal stretcher bar in the centres of the rails.

9 The mortises for the stretcher are the same size as those for the rails, allowing a similar amount for the wedges. Good accurate joints are required for this assembly to ensure a rigid base for the table.

10 Assemble the stretcher to the rails and set aside. Then make the supporting frame for the top. Mark up all the components carefully to avoid confusion at the construction stage – each leg must be fitted individually to the table top.

11 The supporting frame is mortised and tenoned together, having three cross rails to span the laminated top and hold it flat, so make absolutely sure that the frame is not twisted. No wedges are used for these smaller tenons – they are simply glued and clamped together.

12 The longitudinal bearers of the frame extend beyond the outer cross rails, to provide full support for the table ends. Cut small bevels on the ends of each bearer to remove the bottom corners. Then glue and clamp the frame together, making sure that it is square.

13 The tenon at the top of each leg measures 50 x 50mm (2 x 2in) in section, being bare-faced on the inner edge. The shoulders locate under the supporting frame members. Add the thickness of the table top to the depth of the frame members to establish the length of the tenons.

14 Centralize the assembled supporting frame on the underside of the table top. Attach it with a couple of screws at each corner, then place each leg in turn in its corner of the frame as shown. Mark the positions of the mortises on the top, then remove the frame, marking it first so that you can replace it in the same position.

15 Use a try square to transfer the mortise positions to the upper face of the top and scribe around the edges of the cutouts. Use a spade bit or auger mounted in a drill to remove the bulk of the waste, then pare down the sides so that the tenons are a sliding fit.

16 Clamp each leg upright and cut two small slots in the top of the tenon for the wedges. The slots should be no more than 25mm (1in) deep – the thickness of the table top – to avoid weakening the tenons more than is necessary.

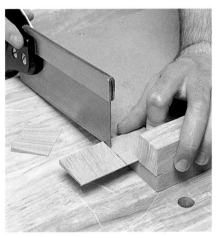

17 Fashion a wedge-shaped section of wood from an offcut of the table top material, using a bandsaw or circular saw to achieve a sharp feather edge. Note the grain direction. Using a tenon saw, cut the strip into eight 50mm (2in) wedges.

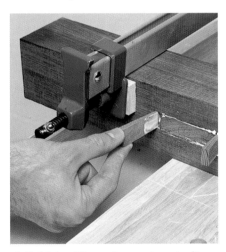

18 Make 12 smaller wedges to fit the cross rail and stretcher tenons in the same way. Glue each pair of legs and corresponding cross rail in turn, keeping them flat and free from any twisting. Clamp them so that the assembly is square, insert the small wedges and tap them in.

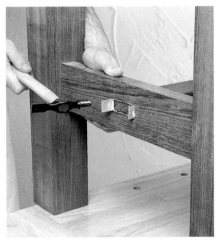

19 Stand the two ends upright on a flat surface. Slip the support frame over the tops of the legs to position them correctly, then insert the connecting stretcher between the rails. Place the table top over the tenons, square up the legs and tap in the wedges. Leave both sections to dry before proceeding to the next step. Leave the top in position to keep the assembly square while the glue dries, then remove it for the final attachment.

20 Apply glue to the tenons at the tops of the legs, replace the table top and hammer in the wedges, using a small block of wood to protect the ends and keep them straight. Note the direction of the slots in the tenons – this prevents the wedges from applying pressure to the longitudinal grain of the table top. When the glue is dry, cut the excess from the wedges and sand the tops of the legs flush with the surface.

SETTLE

"SETTLE" IS AN OLD NAME for a wooden seat with a high back and raised arm rests. This version reflects the early origins of the concept by using wedged-through tenons, one of the earliest carpentry techniques, dating from medieval times. It departs from tradition, however, in the gently curved profile of the ends, which give a more contemporary feel to the whole design. The example shown was made from wide boards of sweet chestnut, a much neglected wood often mistaken for oak, with its attractive grain figure and delicate pale brown colour.

Practical tip

Position the seat slightly lower if you want to add an upholstered cushion, maintaining the overall height above the floor of 460mm (18in).

Construction

The design employs a minimum of simple joints, yet it is strong and rigid. The wedged-through tenons are not glued, and the whole assembly can be taken apart whenever required. The seat can be made to any width, but these dimensions are suitable for a two-seater.

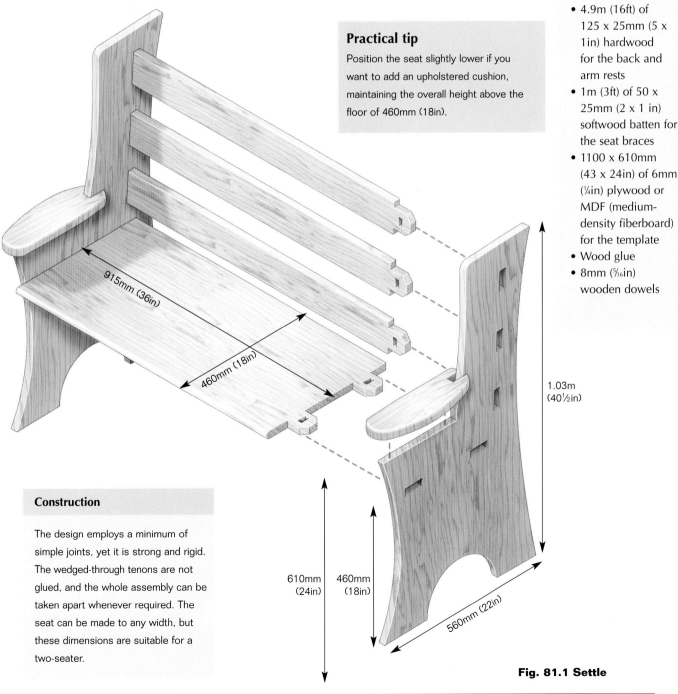

915mm (36in)

460mm (18in)

1.03m (40½in)

610mm (24in)

460mm (18in)

560mm (22in)

Fig. 81.1 Settle

**Fig. 82.1
End
profile**

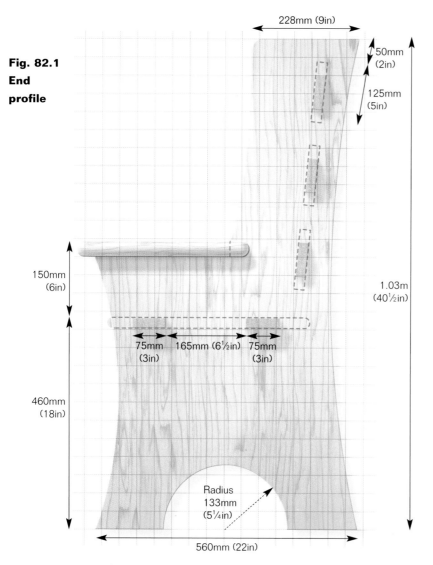

228mm (9in)

50mm (2in)

125mm (5in)

1.03m (40½in)

150mm (6in)

75mm (3in) 165mm (6½in) 75mm (3in)

460mm (18in)

Radius 133mm (5¼in)

560mm (22in)

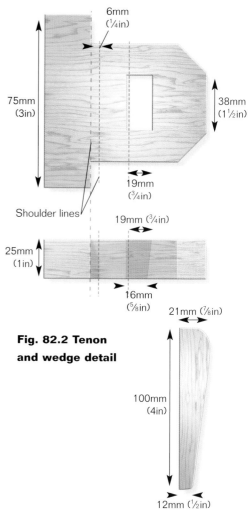

6mm (¼in)

75mm (3in)

38mm (1½in)

19mm (¾in)

Shoulder lines

19mm (¾in)

25mm (1in)

16mm (⅝in)

Fig. 82.2 Tenon and wedge detail

21mm (⅞in)

100mm (4in)

12mm (½in)

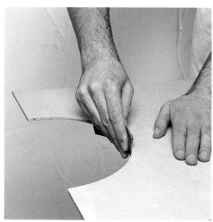

1 Make a full-sized template for the end profile from 6mm (¼in) plywood or MDF. Use the scale drawing provided (figure 82.1), plotting the outline on a scaled-up grid to transfer the shape. Mark and cut out the mortise positions at the same time.

2 Begin by edge jointing all the components for the seat and the ends. Rout grooves in the edges of the boards and clamp them together with loose tongues for extra strength. Note the straight batten clamped over the work to keep it flat as the sash cramps (clamps) are tightened.

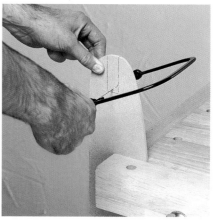

3 The arm rests are laminated from a double thickness of wood. Make a template of suitable shape, cutting a 50 x 25mm (2 x 1in) locating slot in it. Cut out and shape four pieces, using a router fitted with a follower cutter. Square off the ends of the locating slots.

4 Glue the arm rest pairs together and set aside for the glue to dry before shaping. Note the small block of wood inserted into the slot to keep the two pieces aligned. Remove the excess glue, sand smooth and round off the edges.

5 Cut the ends roughly to shape, slightly oversize, and pin the template to each in turn. Mark through the template to transfer the positions of the cutouts for the tenons on to the workpiece so that both ends are identical.

6 Use a router fitted with a follower cutter to trim the ends to their final shape. The bearing on the end of the cutter follows the curved template beneath the work, which should be clamped firmly to the bench.

7 To make the cutouts, drill a hole at each end of the slot and join them with a jigsaw to remove the waste. Cut just inside the line. Pin the template to the reverse of the work, then use the router to trim the slot to size, as in the previous step.

8 Square the ends of each slot with a bevelled chisel. A good tight fit to suit the thickness of the tenons will ensure a rigid construction when the latter are wedged in place. Ease the slots with a piece of sandpaper and a wooden block of the right size until a good sliding fit is achieved.

9 The seat is housed in a groove for maximum support. Clamp a straightedge to the inner face of each end to guide the router, aligning the groove exactly with the slots. A depth of 6mm (¼in) is sufficient for the housing. When the wedges on the seat are drawn up tight, the seat should fit securely in the housings.

10 Rout a similar 6mm (¼in) deep groove in the underside of each arm rest to fit over the ends. Square off the end of the groove with a chisel to suit the exact length of the side location. Then radius the edges and sand smooth.

11 Drill two holes for 8mm (⁵⁄₁₆in) dowels in the edge of each end that supports the arm rest. Insert the dowel centre-points and slot the arm rest over the end piece, pressing down to mark the corresponding hole positions on the underside of the arm rest. Drill the holes.

12 Make a template for the tenons, using the diagram (figure 82.2) as a guide. Note the alternative shoulder lines that allow the same template to be used for both seat and back rails, the former being longer by 6mm (¼in). For the rails, the shoulders are flush to the inside face of the sides.

13 Cut the tenons on the ends of the back rails, and mark out the small slots for the wedges. Set the shoulder lines 915mm (36in) apart on each rail to the internal width of the seat. Trim the corners of the tenons, as shown, and sand them smooth.

14 Use the same template to mark out the tenons on the seat, but note how the shoulders are set forward by 6mm (¼in) to allow for the housing groove that receives the seat. Scribe along the shoulder lines and cut the ends carefully to shape with a jigsaw.

15 Drill out the slots for the wedges and remove the waste. Make each slot 16mm (⅝in) wide, then use a chisel to form the small bevel shown in the diagram. Mark the bevel on the side of the tenon as a guide to keep the chisel at the correct angle.

16 Make ten wedges from offcuts (scraps) of wood, following the dimensions given. The angle of each wedge should fit the slot in its tenon exactly. Shape one wedge first, check for accuracy, then use it as a pattern for the others.

17 Before assembly, glue and screw two 50 x 25mm (2 x 1in) battens to the underside of the seat to stiffen it and help prevent any deformation of the edge-jointed sections. The battens are 25mm (1in) shorter than the width of the seat at each end.

18 Assemble the settle, easing each tenon into its slot and inserting the wedges temporarily to hold it together while you add the components. An assistant is useful at this stage to support the other end of the seat and rails.

19 Insert the rails with the slots facing forward, as shown, and tap all the wedges home. Because the slots are inset slightly from the outer faces of the seat ends, the wedging action will tighten the whole assembly until it is completely rigid.

20 Finally, attach the arm rests, locating them with the dowels and tapping them firmly into place. Use a block of scrap wood to protect the surface.

CONSERVATORY BENCH

THIS PROJECT WOULD LOOK PERFECTLY AT HOME in a conservatory or garden room. Its slatted construction allows plenty of light to pass through and around it, while keeping the weight down so that it is easily moved. For all that, it is remarkably strong, and being of generous length, it could even be used as a day bed if provided with a few loose cushions. It is made of iroko, a naturally hard and durable wood, so it would be equally suitable for use outdoors as a garden bench during the summer.

Materials

- 3.6m (12ft) of 50 x 50mm (2 x 2in) hardwood for the legs
- 10.7m (35ft) of 75 x 22mm (3 x ⅞in) hardwood for the rails
- 2.45m (8ft) of 65 x 19mm (2½ x ¾in) hardwood for the large slats
- 14.7m (48ft) of 19 x 19mm (¾ x ¾in) hardwood for the small slats
- 4m (13ft) of 38 x 25mm (1½ x 1in) hardwood for the seat battens
- 1.4m x 900mm (55 x 35in) of 12mm (½in) birch plywood for the seat
- 8 100mm (4in) bolts and cross-dowels
- Wood glue
- 8mm (⁵⁄₁₆in) wooden dowels
- 25mm (1in) and 38mm (1½in) wood screws

Fig. 87.1 Conservatory bench

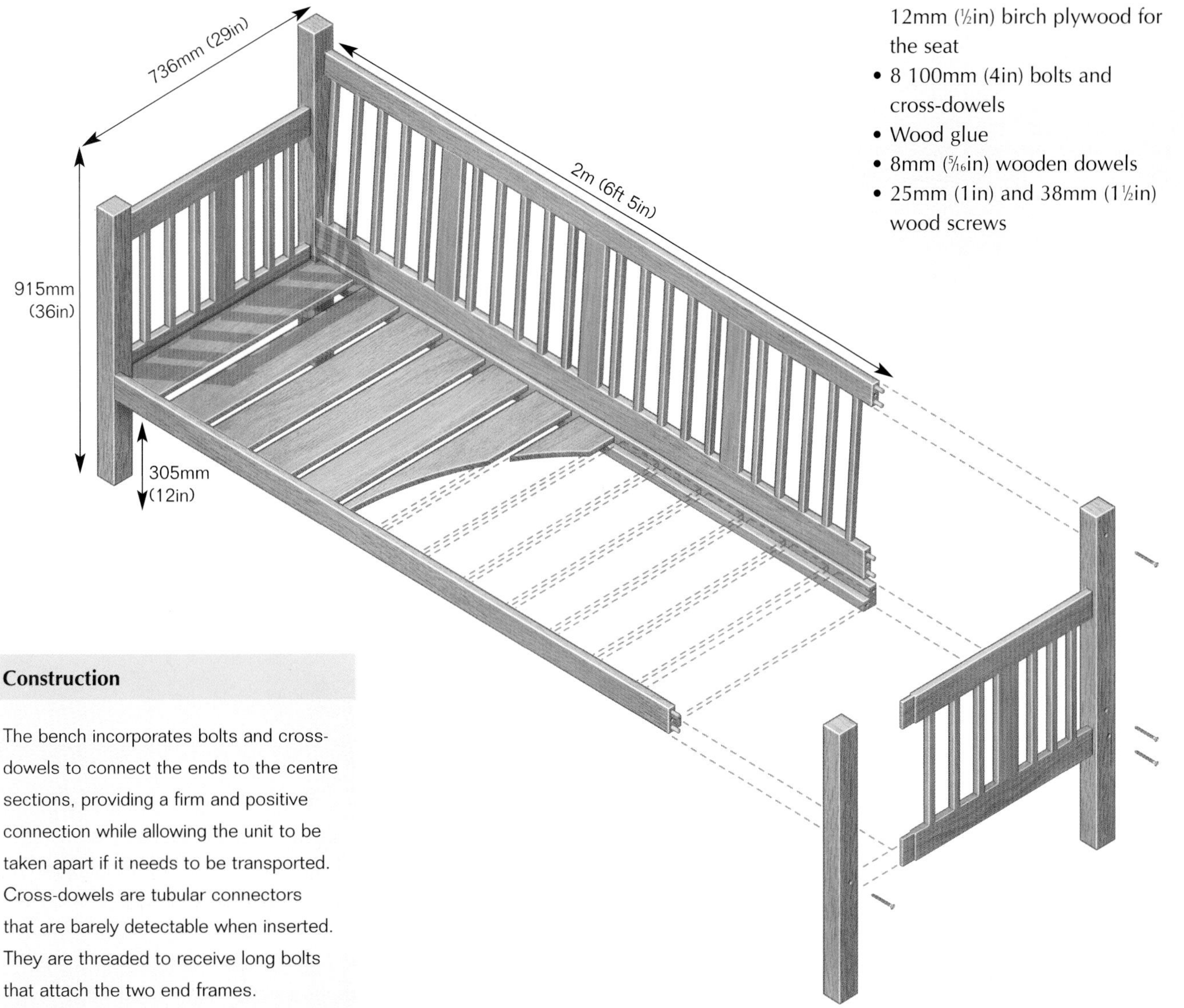

736mm (29in)

2m (6ft 5in)

915mm (36in)

305mm (12in)

Construction

The bench incorporates bolts and cross-dowels to connect the ends to the centre sections, providing a firm and positive connection while allowing the unit to be taken apart if it needs to be transported. Cross-dowels are tubular connectors that are barely detectable when inserted. They are threaded to receive long bolts that attach the two end frames.

Fig. 88.1 End profile

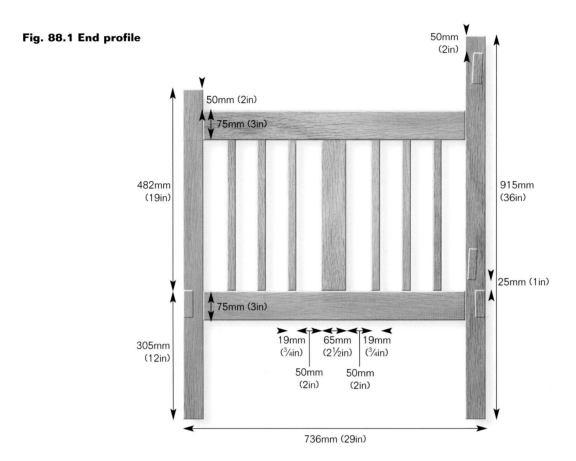

50mm (2in)

50mm (2in)

75mm (3in)

482mm (19in)

915mm (36in)

25mm (1in)

75mm (3in)

19mm (¾in)   65mm (2½in)   19mm (¾in)

50mm (2in)   50mm (2in)

305mm (12in)

736mm (29in)

1 Make the end frames first. Cut the legs to length, and scribe 12mm (½in) wide mortises with a mortise gauge as shown. Do this with the front and back legs clamped together, flush at the bottom. The diagram (figure 88.1) gives the dimensions required to set out the end frames.

2 Cut the mortises 32mm (1¼in) deep to leave enough room for the connecting bolts. Pare the ends and sides of each mortise true and square, making sure that the bottom is free of obstructions.

3 Set out the tenons on the cross rails, then clamp the rails together in pairs to mark out the mortises for the vertical slats. The wider, central slat is positioned first, then the smaller slats are placed at equal intervals along the rail.

4 Cut the tenons on the rails, and pare down with a shoulder plane for a good square fit in the mortises. Note that the shoulders only run along the wide faces of each rail. The mortise is the full height of the rail in this case.

5 Cut all the mortises in the rails. You can drill to a depth of 32mm (1¼in) and chisel them out, as shown, but there are a lot of them, so if you have a drill stand or, even better, a mortise attachment for a power drill, it's well worth setting up to do this.

6 Cut the tenons on all the slats and pare them to fit, clamping them together so that you can true up (square) all the shoulders in one operation. This ensures that all will be drawn up tight when the frame is glued together.

7 Before assembling the frame, sand all the surfaces that will be difficult to clean up later – it saves a lot of time and trouble.

8 Glue all the slats and fit them to the rails to make a sub-assembly that can be connected to the legs in one operation. It should not be necessary to wait for the glue to dry in this instance; the assembly should be rigid enough to proceed to the next step.

9 Clamp each frame together with a pair of sash cramps (clamps), keeping them flat on the bench to prevent any twisting. Wipe off any excess glue and continue with the slatted back section of the bench while the glue dries. Lay one frame on top of the other to make sure they are identical in size.

Practical tip

This project is made up in stages from several sub-assemblies. As each one is completed, it can be easier to finish and apply a coat of sealer before constructing the finished bench.

10 Clamp the bottom rail in a vice and insert all the vertical slats. If you have worked accurately and methodically, all the narrow slats and all the wider slats should be interchangeable. Double check each one before applying glue, however, in case it should need easing slightly.

11 Attach the top rail, starting at one end of the assembly and gradually working your way along. You will find it very useful to have an assistant support the free end. Tap the rail into place with a rubber mallet, locating all the slats before applying the cramps. Make sure the ends are aligned and the assembly is square, and leave to dry.

12 Mark the positions of the connecting bolts and dowels on the inner faces of the end frames. Note that the back is inclined outward at the top to provide a more comfortable seating position. The 50mm (2in) legs allow an angle of about 3 degrees within their width, which makes all the difference. Use a bevel gauge to set out the positions of the back rails.

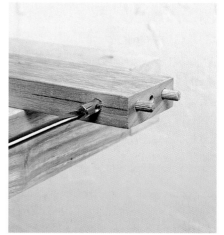

13 Each end of each rail is fitted with two 8mm (5⁄16in) diameter wooden dowels to locate it accurately and prevent it from twisting when the bolt is tightened. The central hole is drilled to suit the diameter of the bolt. Use centre-points to mark the hole positions on each rail – note the block of scrap wood clamped to the bench to hold the rail square.

14 Clamp the rails horizontally to drill the holes in the ends. The holes for the connecting bolts should be drilled to a full 75mm (3in) depth to allow plenty of clearance. Get someone to help you by standing to one side to check that your drill bit is truly horizontal.

15 Drill a hole for the cross-dowel, intersecting the bolt hole, and insert the cross-dowel from beneath the rail. Note the slot in the end of the dowel, which is used to align the hole to receive the bolt. When the slot is parallel to the sides of the rail, the bolt should enter the dowel easily.

16 Countersink the holes for the bolts in the outer faces of the legs so that the heads sit just below the surface. Align the wooden dowels, tap the end frames into place and tighten the bolts with the key provided. The result is a discreet and immensely strong connection.

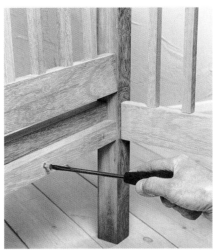

17 Cut two battens to the full length of the front and back rails, and screw them in place to support the seat. The seat can be made of any suitable sheet material – in this case, 12mm (½in) plywood strips were used to provide a degree of flexibility.

18 The two endmost strips should be notched to fit around the legs. Note that the top edges of the plywood have been radiused with a rounding-over cutter to prevent splinters from catching on the upholstered seat cushions. Sand all the strips smooth before fixing.

19 Screw the plywood strips to the battens, using a block of wood to ensure regular spacing. Make sure that the screw heads are countersunk well to prevent them from snagging on the cushion material.

GLOSSARY

Some of the less familiar woodworking terms encountered in this book are listed here.

bare-faced A type of tenon joint where the shoulder is formed on only one face of the tenon.

batten A length of timber (lumber), usually square in section, for joining or strengthening.

baulk A squared log from which smaller sections of timber are converted in the sawmill.

bench hook A portable stop, often home-made, which fits over the edge of a bench for steadying the workpiece.

bevel The angled edge or end of a piece of wood – measured and marked with a bevel gauge.

biscuit A small flat lozenge-shaped dowel for edge or corner jointing – fitted with a biscuit jointer.

botanical name The Latin name that uniquely identifies the genus and species of timber.

burr (burl) The part of a tree with twisted and complex grain formation, prized for its decorative appearance.

carcass The basic box assembly of any construction, such as a cabinet or shelving unit.

chamfer To remove the sharp corner of a section of wood and produce a smooth bevelled edge. *(vb & n)*

chuck The adjustable jaws of a power drill or hand brace.

clearance hole A hole drilled through a panel to allow clearance for the shank of a wood screw.

conversion A method of cutting wood from the baulk to produce boards for woodworking.

counterbore A cylindrical hole at the top of the clearance hole to recess the head of a screw below the surface.

cross-dowel A threaded metal rod inserted across the grain of a wooden member to receive a connecting bolt.

density The relative weight of a substance, expressed as kilograms per cubic metre, or pounds per cubic foot.

dowel A cylindrical length of wood used for connecting a joint, sometimes fluted to allow good adhesion.

face and edge marks Pencil marks to identify the square and straight edges of a length of wood before working it.

flute A semi-circular groove in a piece of wood; also, the description of the cutting tool to produce it.

follower (fence) A circular fitting for the base of a router used to follow the edge of a template.

growth rings Layers of annual growth in the tree, clearly visible in cross section.

hardwood Wood from broad-leaved trees, usually harder and more close-grained than coniferous softwoods, ideal for fine finishing or joinery.

haunch A shortened section of a tenon, formed at the outside edge of a joint to prevent twisting.

hockey stick (corner bead) A moulding used to trim the edges of a panel, with a J-shaped section in the profile of a hockey-stick to produce a finished edge.

horn The end of frame member in a door or panel, which projects past the mortise for added strength.

housing A grooved joint, square in section, which receives the end of another component.

jig A woodworking aid for controlling the tool or locating the workpiece, for added safety or accuracy.

kiln-dried Seasoned timber that has been dried in the kiln to a low moisture content of approximately 10%

laminate A thin layer of wood or other material, used for forming curves or building up a decorative surface. *(vb & n)*

liming wax	Finishing wax that imparts a delicate white colour to the grain of the wood.
MDF	Medium-density fiberboard – all-purpose sheet material, available in a range of thicknesses with a smooth sanded surface, suitable for home woodworking projects of all kinds.
mitre	Halving the angle of a corner joint where two members intersect: in a right angle, two 45 degree angles. *(vb & n)*
moisture content	A measure of how dry a sample of wood may be – low moisture content means the wood is stable and well-seasoned.
mortise	The square socket that receives a tenon for the classic woodworker's mortise and tenon joint. The mortise is the female part of the joint.
moulding	Decorative profiled edge of a length of wood, formed either by hand or with machine tools.
movement	The tendency of wood to shrink or expand with the changing atmospheric conditions of its surroundings.
nominal	The size of a section of wood after sawing, before machining further to an exact dimension.
pare	To remove thin layers of wood by hand with a flat chisel blade.
pilot hole	A hole drilled to receive the threaded end of a wood screw, to assist location and prevent the wood from splitting.
plinth (kick)	A raised base of a cupboard or floor unit, usually detachable.
prepared	Describes planed timber with smooth faces and square edges.
profile	Any shape produced from a square blank of timber.
profile cutter	A special cutter fitted to a router, used to follow a template for reproducing a particular profile.
rail	The upper or lower horizontal member in a door or panel.
rebate (rabbet)	To cut a rectangular, stepped recess along the edge of a section of wood.
relish	A cutaway section of a tenon joint to avoid the edge or corner of a frame, and thus avoid weakening the joint.

scribe	To mark or shape the end of a section of wood to fit around a moulding or profile for a neat joint. *(vb & n)*
shooting board (stop)	A home-made jig used with a bench plane to square the end or the edges of a length of wood.
shorts/short ends (cuts)	Shorter lengths of wood as sold by a timber yard at lower cost, often suitable for home woodworking projects.
shoulder	The edge of a tenon joint that mates with the surface of another component, keeping it square.
softwood	Relatively inexpensive, general-purpose timber, from pine or other coniferous trees.
sole plate	The smooth base plate of a plane, which makes contact with the wood when in use.
stretcher	Part of a wooden frame, usually between two rails, to maintain a fixed distance between them.
TCT	Tungsten-carbide tipped: better quality, but more expensive, cutters and sawblades.
template	A pattern, usually of wood, used as a guide to form complex shapes or for repetitive, accurate work.
tenon	The male section of a mortise and tenon joint.
tongue	A thin strip of wood that slots into a matching groove in the faces of a joint, which strengthens that joint.
veneer	Very thin slices of wood for high quality decorative work.
vice	A good-quality vice on a sturdy bench is an essential piece of the woodworker's equipment. Vices are generally fixed to a bench on the right-hand end.
wire wool	An abrasive that cuts down the wood surface. It is sometimes used with wax as a lubricant.

SUPPLIERS

United Kingdom

Axminster Power Tool Centre
Chard Street
Axminster
Devon EX13 5HU
Tel: 01297 33656
Hand and power tools.

Blumson Fine Timber
36–38 River Road
Barking
Essex IG11 0DN
Tel: 020 8594 5175
Timber (lumber).

Chestergate Wood Supplies Ltd.
Porron Street
Portwood, Stockport
Greater Manchester SK1 2JD
Timber.

Crown Fasteners and Fixings Ltd.
Watermill House
Restmor Way, Hackridge
Surrey SM6 7AH
Tel: 020 8773 3993
Hardware.

Dewalt
210 Bath Road
Slough
Berkshire SL1 3YD
Tel: 01753 567055
Power tools.

Foxell and James
Farringdon Road
London EC1M 3JB
Tel: 020 7405 0152
Finishing products.

FR Shadbolt & Sons Ltd.
North Circular Road
South Chingford
London E4 8PZ
Tel: 020 8527 6441
Veneers.

James Latham
Leeside Wharf
Mount Pleasant Hill
Clapton E5
Tel: 020 8806 3333
Timber.

John Boddy's Wood and Tool Store
Riverside Sawmills
Boroughbridge
North Yorkshire YO51 9LJ
Tel: 01423 322370
Timber.

Machin Bros. Ltd.
79 Sceptre Road
Bethnal Green
London E2 0JU
Tel: 020 7790 3575
Veneers.

North Wales Timber Ltd.
Industrial Estate
Pinfold Lane
Buckley
Flintshire CH7 3PL
Timber.

Record Tools Ltd.
Parkway Works
Kettlebridge Road
Sheffield S9 3BL
Tel: 0114 244 9066
Hand tools.

Spear & Jackson
Neill Tools Ltd.
Atlas Way
Atlas North
Sheffield S4 7QQ
Tel: 0114 261 4242
Tools and saw specialist.

Stanley Tools UK Ltd.
Beighton Road East
Drakehouse
Sheffield S20 7JZ
Tel: 0114 276 8888
Tools.

West and Heaton Timber Ltd.
4 North Back Lane
Bridlington
East Yorkshire YO16 5BA
Timber.

Winther Browne & Co.
Nobel Road
Eley Estate
Edmonton
London N18 3DX
Tel: 020 8803 3434
Fine wood carvings and mouldings.

Woodfit Ltd.
Kem Mill
Whittle-le-Woods
Chorley
Lancashire PR6 7EA
Tel: 01257 266421
Furniture fittings and trimmings.

Y Goldburg & Sons
3–5 Waterloo Road
Uxbridge
Middlesex UB8 2QX
Tel: 01895 253491
Timber.

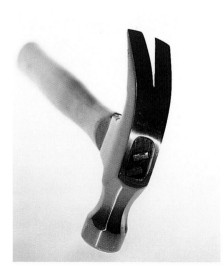

United States
California Redwood Association
405 Enfrente Drive
Suite 200
Novato, CA 94949
Tel: (415) 382-0662

Colonial Hardwoods Inc.
7953 Cameron Brown Ct.
Springfield, VA 22153
Tel: (703) 451-9217

Diamond Machining Technology Inc.
85 Hayes Memorial Drive
Malborough, MA 01752
Tel: (800) 666-4368
Woodworking tools.

North Atlantic Timber Corporation
South Road
Chilmark, MA 0235
Tel: (508) 696-8939

Southern Pine Council
P.O. Box 641700
Kenner, LA, 70064-1700
Tel: (504) 443-4464

Australia
Anagote Timbers
144 Renwick Street
Marrickville
New South Wales 2204
Tel: 02 9558 8444

Trend Timbers Pty Ltd.
Cunneen Street, McGraths Hill
New South Wales 2756
Tel: 02 4577 5277

The Wood Works
8 Railway Road, Meadowbank
New South Wales 2114
Tel: 02 9807 7244

Veneers
37 Alexandra Road
East Ringwood
Victoria 3135
Tel: 03 9870 8733

The publisher would like to thank the following individuals and suppliers for lending equipment and their help with photography.

Bob Cleveland
111 Stillingfleet Road
London SW13 9AF

Andrew Gillmore
For making the three-legged chair project.

Woodfit
For the loan of fixtures and fittings.

Stanley UK Tools Ltd.
For the loan of tools.

Spear & Jackson
For the loan of saws.

Dewalt
For the loan of power tools.

Volume
21 St. Alban's Place, London N1 0NX
Tel: 020 7359 0224

Record Tools Ltd.
For the loan of chisels.

Fothergills
79 Salmon Lane
Limehouse, London E14 7NA
Tel: 020 7790 7774

Chromacolor by Perstorp
Perstorp Customer Hotline
Tel: 01325 303303

The Old Tool Chest
41 Cross Street
London N1 2BB
Tel: 020 7359 9313

James Latham
Leeside Wharf
Mount Pleasant Hill, London E5
Tel: 020 8806 3333

Grahams Hi Fi
Canonbury Yard
190a New North Road
London N1 7BS
Tel: 020 7226 5500

Gill Wing Cookshop
190 Upper Street
London N1 1RQ
Tel: 020 7226 5392

Axminster Power Tool Centre
Chard Street
Axminster, Devon EX13 5HU

Mr Wright
Blumsom Timber Centre

Liz Boddy
John Boddy's Wood and Tool Store

Justin Browne
Winther Browne & Co.
Fine Wood Carvings & Mouldings

Paul Machin
Machin Bros. Ltd.

Suzanna Tabor
FR Shadbolt & Sons

Vin Vara
The Tool Shop
97 Lower Marsh, London SE1
Tel: 020 7207 2077

Drew Geldart
Spear & Jackson
Neill Tools Ltd.

Record Tools Ltd.

INDEX

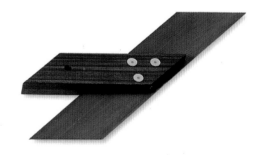